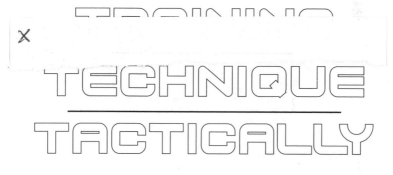

TRAINING

TECHNIQUE

TACTICALLY

Mark Nicole

REEDSWAIN
PUBLISHING

Library of Congress Cataloging - in - Publication Data

Training Technique Tactically
Nicole, Mark

ISBN No. 1-59164-081-4
Lib. of Congress Catalog No. 2004093485
© 2004

Art Direction, Layout and Editing
Bryan Beaver

Photographs
Robyn McNeil
Richard Kentwell

Diagrams
Dan Spollen

Printed by
DATA REPRODUCTIONS
Auburn, Michigan

Reedswain Publishing
612 Pughtown Road
Spring City, PA 19475
800.331.5191
www.reedswain.com
info@reedswain.com

For three people willing to understand me:
Susan, Dustin & Dillon
Thank You.

Contents

Foreword

The concept of this book is to promote the growth of developing soccer players based upon training sessions which have both a technical and tactical objective. The intention is to develop the player's ability to deal technically with the ball while in a problem solving situation, all the while playing at the highest possible speed and decision making function.

The book by design is structured with both experienced and less experienced individuals in mind. Numerous and varied teaching opportunities will present themselves and the requirements of each particular game will steer the play into the training objective. The high degree of structure is a vehicle by which the trainer should utilize his own creativity to achieve his vision of what player development means. Suggestions to the reader are to adjust the field size to your team's ability and physical strength. Avoid forcing the progressions or times allocated to each activity or training game and adjust touch number requirements and the like based upon the level of the players.

The structure of the training sessions is by intention extremely manageable for the trainer to set up and move through. Much must be accomplished in a small amount of time. The flow of each session from activity to activity must be smooth and efficient. Interesting and progressively more involved problem solving activities assure the desired involvement of the players at every level on a particular team. Players within a team environment now have an increased chance of reaching their full individual potential.

The best of luck to you,

Mark

Technique and Tactics*

Most would agree the modern game continues to evolve into one of increased speed of play in attack, immediate transition and the increased pressure of playing efficiently in decreased space with less time. As a consequence, much higher levels of competence are being expected of players as individuals and as a collective unit. These levels are of course technical and tactical in nature as well as extremely demanding psychologically and physically.

Youth training sessions now must incorporate less exclusive teaching of technique in preparation for this phenomenon. The drilling of technique without adding difficulty and pressure is myopic. What is taught must be match-related to foster a more complete development of the young player. This is not to profess that practicing a specific technique in isolation outside of the moving game is counterproductive. This type of training is necessary, but should be made more realistic as soon as possible.

The challenge now becomes how to effectively present, demonstrate and teach advanced technical training topics within a format that incorporates other facets of the game. To succeed, training must be stimulating for the players, manageable for the coach and relevant to the match. For example, basic concepts such as looking up field to play an early pass forward to feet and striking the ball with the instep must be taught simultaneously.

The technical ability becomes an acquired skill enabling the player to solve tactical soccer problems more efficiently which in turn will ease to some degree the psychological burden with which developing players are confronted. Individual confidence and composure on the ball will manifest into collective cohesiveness of the group. Through this cycle players will continue to influence one another in a self-directed, player-coaching-player environment. This facilitates personal growth within the team structure, increasing the probability of the individual reaching his or her full potential as a soccer player.

*From an article by the author published in the Soccer Journal, July/August 2002

Over time this culture becomes the accepted norm and each player benefits immensely from the combined experience. The message here is training must incorporate both technical and tactical areas of focus in concert with one another. If structured correctly this vision can be offered to players at an early age.

To institute this type of mindset, it is important to illustrate the difference between two commonly used terms and approaches, these being "tactics" and "small sided games". Team tactics are the framework by which the collective group attacks and defends in specific situations and locations on the field. Playing direct versus the patience of the counterattacking team is a pertinent example.

This type of knowledge at this level should be discussed and demonstrated as briefly as possible to orient the group to operate within a few general guidelines, setting the stage for the more important matter of teaching individual tactics. Learning to understand the problems and solutions of playing out of pressure near the touchline against even numbers is vastly more important at this stage than to understand the game plan is to stroke a long flighted ball from defending third to attacking third and chase. There must be a separation of learning how to win games versus how to play the game correctly from an early age.

A small-sided game played without a specific technical and tactical focus becomes an exercise in playing a game to justify its own title. Without specified and understandable teaching topics, what is there to be learned? A more directed methodology would be the utilization of training games to elicit the desired behavior from the players, again as individuals and collectively. Various tactical elements can be identified and presented in a forum that provides the trainer with a plethora of teaching opportunities. The proximity and small numbers assure that all will see and hear. There are also ample chances to repeat positive and correct match-related solutions in the correct sized area of the field where the training topic occurs. It then becomes important to relate the issues learned back to the general team playing guidelines.

Within this framework the players become stimulated and in turn have the confidence to experiment and partake in alternative solutions to the problem. The willingness to fearlessly take risk in the attack is a prime and desirable example of a player who has the confidence to deal with the challenges of the situation. The individuals become self-assured and more mature, freeing themselves to experiment with new self-taught solutions.

The crux of all this lies hidden within the ability of the trainer to design sessions that continually teach and recreate an identifiable technical and tactical topic utilizing small player numbers. Building to a team versus team training game on full goals is the objective. This should be considered a worthy endeavor that will indeed take considerable time and patience from all participants. Over time a multitude of rewards will become apparent to the teacher and the tasks required to enjoy them will be vastly outweighed by the pleasure of the experience.

The Exercises

Attacking 1v1 with the Dribble

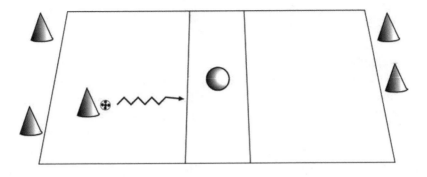

Objectives:
> Technical: Change dribbling direction.
> Tactical: Change of pace during move.

Teaching Points:
> 1. Sharp cuts with the ball.
> 2. Drive defender one direction, attack opposite.
> 3. Once past cut into the defenders running path.

Set up:
> Players: 12 players
> Gear:　16 cones, spare balls
> Field:　30x20 feet with 5 foot middle zone (2 fields)
> Time:　40 minutes

Instructions:
There are 6 players on each field. A defender is positioned in the middle zone and may not chase attackers out of it. The other 5 attacking players are split at each end of the field. To begin the defender must hold hands behind the back. Upon winning a ball the defender dribbles out of the zone and passes to a player on the end. The ball loser becomes the defender. If the attacker beats the defender a pass is made to the end and that player attacks the defender. The game should be high tempo.

Progression:

The middle defender now plays completely live. Players score 1 point for each defender beaten. The games are 5 minutes long. The player on each field with the most points at time wins.

Progression:

When the middle defender is beaten a second defender steps onto the field from the end line. The attacker attempts to beat the second defender over the end line. If the second defender wins the ball the middle zone is attacked. The original attacker may chase until the player reaches the middle zone. If the player gets past the middle defender a third defender will step onto the field on the opposite end. The scoring is the same.

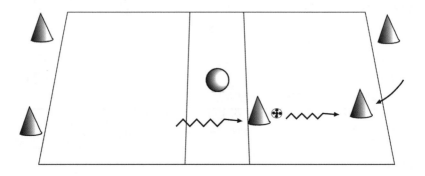

Set up:

      Players: 6v6 with 2 goalkeepers
      Gear: 6 vests, 8 cones, 2 goals
      Field: 60 yards(20-20-20) x Box width
      Time: 5 ten minute games

Instructions:

There are 2 teams of 6 players. One player from each team is positioned in the defensive zone in front of their own goal. The other 10 players begin in the middle zone. The players in the middle must defend in front of their defensive line on the field and may not chase attackers in. The ball must be dribbled into the attacking zone, not passed. The dribbler takes the lone defender on and attempts to score then rejoins the middle group at the end of the play. If the defender wins the ball is dribbled free back to the middle to restart game. A team mate will then become the new defender.

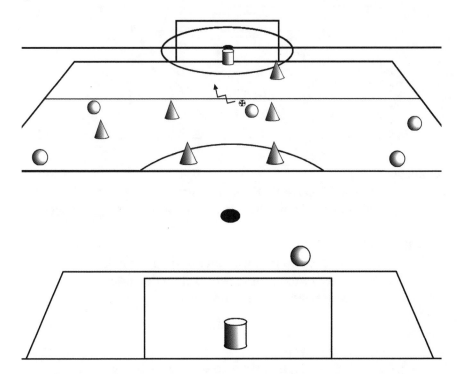

Progression:
The teams may now chase into the attacking zone after the ball has been dribbled in.

Progression:
The players may position themselves anywhere on the field. The ball still must be dribbled over the defensive line.

Creating 1v1 Opportunities to Attack

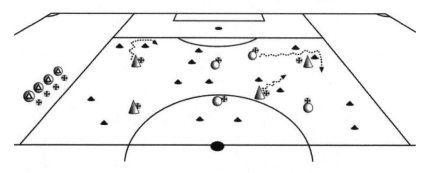

Objectives:
Technical: Receive first touch to attack space on the dribble.
Tactical: Identify lvl situations to create attacking chances.

Teaching Points:
1. Play possession to draw defenders to the ball.
2. Move away from pressure to isolate defender.
3. Play with head up to identify lv1's.

Set up:
Players: 12 players
Gear: 16 cones, 8 vests(2 colors),12 balls
Field: 40 yds by 30 yds
Time: 60 minutes

Instructions:
There are three teams of four players each. All players begin with
their own ball. On the field there are eight five yard wide cone goals
placed randomly. Two teams work while one team rests. Each player
counts the number of goals dribbled through. Play 10 games of 1
minute each. Switch resting teams each game.

Progression:
The first player to dribble through 15 goals wins a point. Play a 10
minute game with brief rest periods.

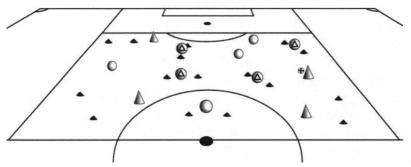

Progression:
Two teams play 4v4. The object is to dribble the ball through one of the eight cone goals for a point. The third team plays as four moving goalkeepers. Their responsibility is to stop either team from dribbling through a goal. They may only defend goals and may not use their hands. The game is continuous after a goal. Play 10 games of 2 minutes each. Switch the goalkeeping team each game.

Progression:
After a goal is scored the defenders immediately become the goalkeeping team and the previous goalkeepers will immediately become the new defenders. Play 10 games of 2 minutes each.

Set up:
>   Players: 12 players, 2 goalkeepers
>   Gear: 8 cones, 8 vests, 2 goals
>   Field: 60 yds by 44 yds divided in 3 zones
>   Time: 30 minutes

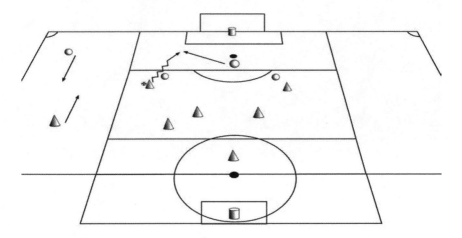

Instructions:
The game is 6v6. There is a 5v5 in the middle zone and one defender from each team in their defensive zone. Play begins in the midfield zone. The ball must be dribbled into the attacking zone for a 1v1. No middle players from either team may enter the attacking/defending zones until the ball goes in on the dribble. After each attack switch both defenders on the fly. If the ball goes over an end line or is saved players retreat to the midfield zone where play is restarted. Play 3 games of 5 minutes each.

Progression:
Players may be positioned anywhere on the field. The ball must still be dribbled into the attacking zone. Play 3 games of 5 minutes each.

Turning 1v1 to Play Forward

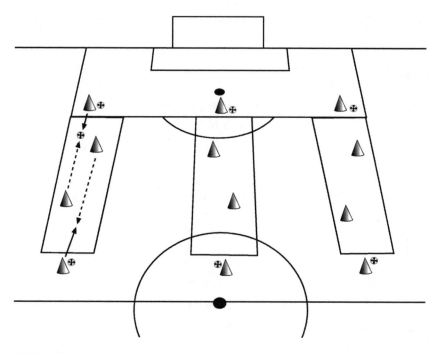

Objectives:
> Technical: Perform shoulder feint before the turn.
> Tactical: Look up-field on the first touch.

Teaching Points:
> 1. Make the feint a shoulder dip.
> 2. Make a moving first touch turn.
> 3. Keep eyes up, looking to pass forward early.

Set up:
> Players: 12 players
> Gear: 12 cones, spare balls
> Field: 25 yds by 10 yds (3 fields)
> Time: 20 minutes

Instructions:
The players are in groups of four on each field. Two players are positioned inside the field. The other two players are positioned one at each end line with a ball each. Each middle player checks to an end

line player to receive a pass and turn with it. The next move is to pass early to the opposite end line player then follow the pass for a 1 2 combination with that player. Alternate doing inside foot and outside foot turns. Play for 2 minutes, then switch.

Set up:

     Players: 12 players
     Gear: 8 cones, 6 vests, spare balls
     Field;   30 yds by 20 yds (2 fields)
     Time: 30 minutes

Instructions:

The game is 3v3. The players compete lvl in the middle of the field with a teammate positioned on each end line.

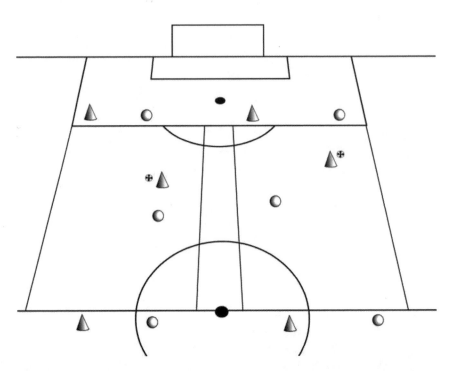

The object of each game is for one of the 1v1 players to check to an end line teammate, receive the pass to feet, then turn and pass to the teammate on the opposite end of the field. The ball must keep moving. If a pass is not on to a middle player, an end line player may play a pass to the other end line player while the middle player is working toward that player to receive a pass and turn. A point is scored when both end line players are used during the same possession. Play games of 1 minute then switch the middle two out. The team with the most games won in 10 minutes gets one point. Play 3 games.

Set up:
Players: 12 players, 2 goalkeepers
Gear: 8 cones, 6 vests, 2 goals
Field: 50 yds by 44 yds with a 10 yd middle zone
Time: 40 minutes

Instructions:
The game is 3v3 in each half. For a team to move the ball from their defensive end to their attacking end a teammate must check back from the attacking end into the middle zone to receive a pass and turn. Defenders may not play live until after the turn. If the ball is lost then regained in the attacking end, it may be taken directly back to goal. Switch attacking directions after a goal or shot. Play 2 games of 10 minutes each.

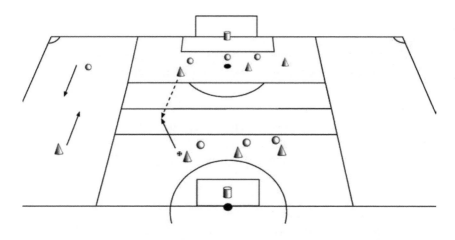

Progression:
Defenders now play completely live in the middle zone. If the defender wins the ball it may be dribbled or passed directly into the attacking end. Play 2 games of 10 minutes each.

Shielding the Ball 1v1

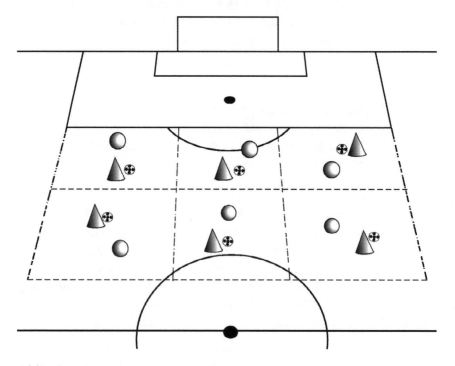

Objective:

    Technical: Keeping ball possession using body position.

    Tactical: Look for dribbling space or possible passes.

Teaching Points:

    1. Maximize distance between defender and ball.

    2. Feel which side of the body is getting pressure.

    3. Touch the ball away from the pressured side.

Set up:

    Players: 12 players

    Gear: 12 cones, 6 vests, balls

    Field: 44 x 30 yards divided into six sections

    Time: 70 minutes

Instructions:

There is a 1v1 in each section. Players may not leave the section they are in. One team has a ball each. The objective of attacking team is to keep all six balls on the field as long as possible. The objective of the defending team is to kick all the balls off the field as soon as possible. A ball losing player may help teammates by receiving passes. Play 10 minutes.

Progression:
The game is 1v1. Games are 1 minute each. The player in possession of the ball at time gets a point for the team. Play six games to determine the winning team. Rotate one team clockwise through the sections while the other team remains static. After this the static team rotates for 6 games. Go through this cycle twice. Rest the players briefly between games. Play 30 minutes.

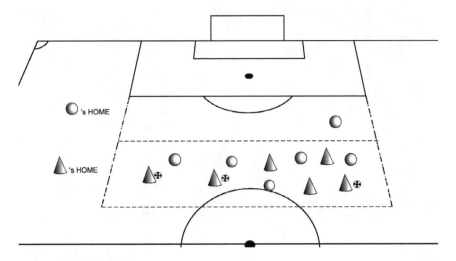

Progression:
One team's home is one half while the opposition's home is the opposite half of the field. There are now three balls. The objective is to keep the ball in the home half. When the ball is won it is transferred to that player's home side. The games are 1 minute each. The team with two balls in their home section at time gets one point. Rotate the 1v1 pairings. Play 15 one minute minutes.

Progression:
All three balls must be in the team's home sections at time for the point to count. Play 15 minutes.

Set up:

       Players: 12 players, 2 goalkeepers
       Gear: 4 cones, 6 vests, 2 goals, balls
       Field: 50 long by 44 wide
       Time: 20 minutes

Instructions:

The game is 6v6 to goal. Players must play a minimum of three touches each time they receive the ball before passing. Shots may be taken at any time.

Receiving 1v1 with Pressure Behind

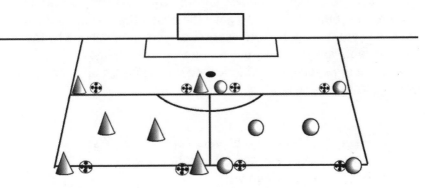

Objectives:
Technical: Receiving a pass while moving toward it.
Tactical: Using the first step as a feint.

Teaching points:
1. Push first touch away from where it was received.
2. Always feint before moving to the passer.
3. Burst to the passer immediately after feint.

Set up:
Players: 12 players
Gear: 8 cones, 8 balls
Field: 40 ft by 40 ft (2 fields)
Time: 60 minutes

Instructions:
Four balls. There are six players on each field. Two players are in the middle. The other four take positions in each corner with a ball each. The middle two make runs to corner players and complete a 1 2 combination then move to a different corner player and repeat. Play 10 games of 1 minute each.

Progression:
Three balls are in play.. The middle two may not play the pass directly back to the corner player who gave them the ball. Balls can never stop dead. Play 20 games of 1 minute each.

Progression:
Two balls. The middle two now play 1v1. They can not pass directly back to the corner player who gave the pass. The ball not in play must be kept moving between corner players until needed by the middle two. Play 30 games of 1 minute each. The player possessing the ball at time gets one point. Rotate the 1v1 match ups and move players from field to field.

Set up:
      Players: 3 teams of 4 players each with 2 GK's
      Gear: 12 vests (3 colors), 4 cones, 2 goals
      Field: 50 yds by 44 yds
      Time: 30 minutes

Instructions:
Two teams play 4v4. The resting team of 4 is positioned one in each corner. After a goal or a dead ball the team that should get the ball must check back toward their own end line and receive a pass from the goal keeper or a corner player. Play 6 games of 5 minutes each.

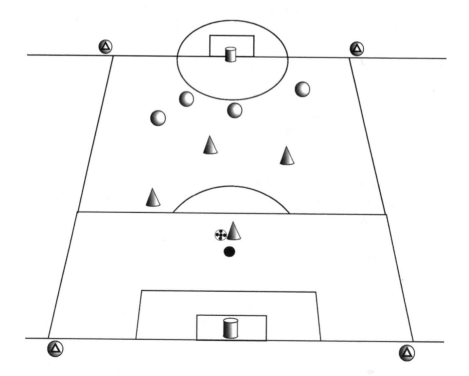

22

Finishing 1v1

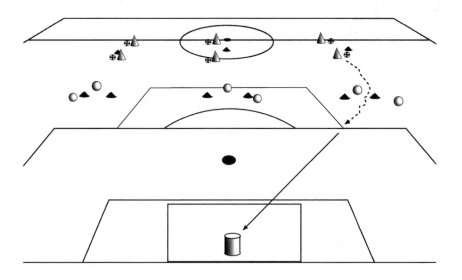

Objective:

    Technical: Shooting off 1vl confrontations.

    Tactical: Creating space for the shot.

Teaching Points:

    1. Run with the ball directly at the defender.

    2. Push the ball past the defender and accelerate.

    3. Head up to pick target, strike ball & follow shot.

Set up:

    Players: 12 players, 1 goalkeeper

    Gear: 9 cones, 6 vests, 1 goal, balls

    Field: half field

    Time: 90 minutes

Instructions:

There are two teams of six players each. There are three, eight feet wide cone goals positioned in a row approximately 30 yards from goal. One team begins as defenders. Two players are positioned at each cone goal. They alternate defending the attackers. The shooting team positions two players at each starting cone which is approximately 15 yards from each cone goal. The game begins with an attacker running at speed at a defender guarding a cone goal. The defender plays passive, is beaten and the shooter plays to the goal-keeper's hands. The next cone goal down the line is attacked. The defenders may not chase through the cone goal once beaten. The attackers continually switch their starting cones. Play 5 minutes with each team as attackers.

Progression:
The defenders and attackers are now live. On a won ball by the defender the play is over and an attack begins at another starting cone. Play 4 games of 5 minutes each. Keep score.

Progression:
Three players from the defending team position themselves inside the "D" on top of the box. The first one in line plays as a second defender going to the ball if a defender is beaten through a cone goal. The next defender prepares to be involved in the next attack. Play 4 games of 5 minutes each.

Progression:
The cone goal defenders may chase the attacker if they are beaten through the cones. Play 4 games of 5 minutes each.

Progression:
Play 6v6 to one goal. The attacking team gets a point for a goal. The defending team becomes the attacking team when it wins a ball and dribbles through one of the three cone goals or receives a pass that went through the cone goal. They then attack the goal. Play 2 games of 10 minutes each.

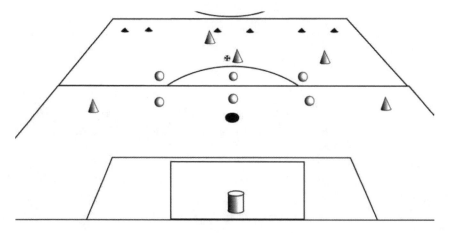

Attacking 2v1 on the Flank

Objective:
> Technical: Play the receiving touch forward.
> Tactical: Choosing to dribble or pass to beat a defender 2v1.

Teaching Points:
> 1. Play first touch with the correct foot.
> 2. Force the wide defender into a bad decision.
> 3. Play at match speed at all times.

Set up:
> Players: 12 Players
> Gear: 16 cones, spare balls
> Field: 15 x 10 yards. 4 fields
> Time: 20 minutes

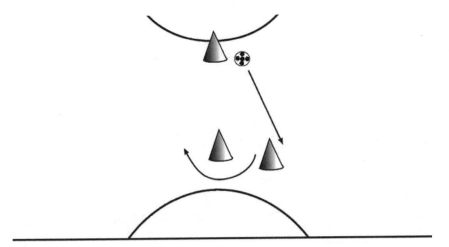

Instructions:
There are three players on each field. They begin in a vertical line.
One player is the passer while the other two are six to eight yards
away. The closer of the two players remains static while the other
makes short curved forward runs to each side of the static player.
This working player passes back to the passer using the correct foot.
The passer must receive and play with the correct foot each time.
Play 10 minutes. Switch positions every minute.

Progression:
The working player must now play first time back to the passer. The static player gives shadow pressure to the working player. The passer plays first time. Play 10 minutes. Switch positions every minute.

Set up:
> Players: 12 Players, 2 Goalkeepers
> Gear: 10 cones, 4 vests, 2 goals, balls
> Field: Half field. 2 marked areas wide.
> Time: 40 minutes

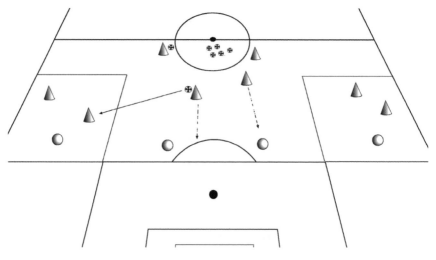

Instructions:
There are four defenders, one on each flank and two in the middle. There are eight attackers, two on each flank and four on the top in pairs. Play begins with a free pass from a pair on top to alternating wide areas. The two wide attackers beat the one defender by dribbling or combining for a 1-2 movement to get behind the defender. The defender may not chase out of the area once beaten. The attacking player dribbles hard toward the end line then drives a serve to the pair running near and far post toward goal from the top. If the flank defender wins the ball, pass immediately to the next pair on top who quickly attack the opposite wide area. Alternate the roles of the players. Switch the keepers. Play 20 minutes.

Progression:
There is now a 3v3 in the middle. The first free pass to the flank is made by the coach from near the center circle. The two flank players

choose to beat the one defender as before or play a 1-2 with one of the three teammates in the middle. The three players from the opposite flank join the attack after the flank defender is beaten on the opposite side. If the defenders win the ball, they pass it to the coach. Alternate the roles of the players. Switch the keepers. Play 20 minutes.

Set up:

Players: 12 Players, 2 goalkeepers
Gear: 10 cones, 8 vests, (2 colors), 2 goals, balls
Field: Half field by 44 yards. Two wide channels
Time: 30 minutes.

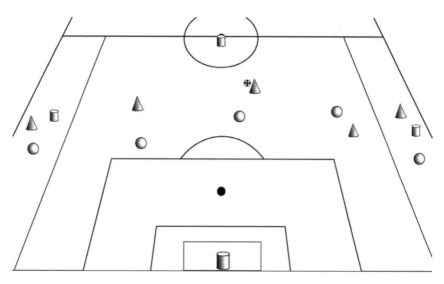

Instructions:

There is a 3v3 in the middle attacking opposite goals. Each team has one teammate in each wide channel. There is also one neutral player in each wide channel who acts as the second attacker for the team with the ball.

The neutral player creates a 2v1 wide with the appropriate player to create an attack down the channel leading to a driven serve. The neutral player changes teams immediately on a turned over ball. A goal is one point. A goal from a ball served from a wide channel is two points. Alternate the roles of the players. Play 3 games of 10 minutes each.

Combination Play 2v1 Near Goal

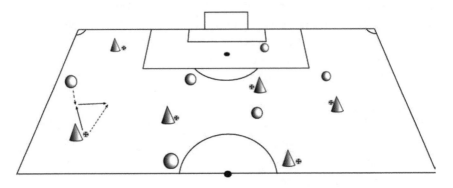

Objectives:

    Technical: Correct foot layoff.

    Tactical: Choosing to release pass or attack.

Teaching Points:

    1. Proper body position to receive pass.

    2. Correct speed/angle of second pass.

    3. Accelerating into space after first pass.

Set up:

    Players: 12 players

    Gear: 4 cones, 6 balls, 6 vests

    Field: half field

    Time: 10 minutes

Instructions:

There are two teams of six players each. One of the teams has a ball for each player. All players are moving freely on the field. The team with the balls looks to play 1-2 combinations with any player from the opposite team. The players without the balls make runs toward the passers to initiate the pass. Switch team roles each 2 minutes.

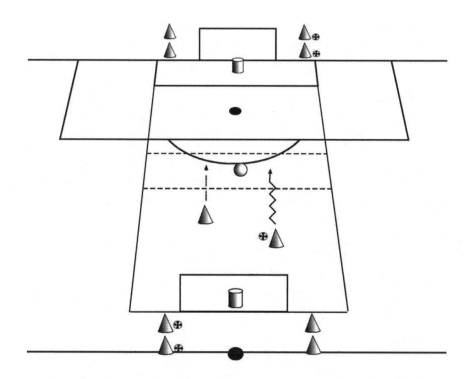

Set up:

      Players: 12 players, 2 goalkeepers
      Gear: 8 cones, 6 vests, 2 goals
      Field: 45 yds long by 20 wide. 5 yd middle zone.
      Time: 60 minutes

Instructions:

There is a defender positioned in the middle zone. The other players are positioned on each end of the field. To begin two attackers dribble into the middle zone and play a one two combination. The defender may not chase out of the zone. After getting the ball back the original attacker takes a dribble then finishes on goal. If the defender cheats the original attacker may dribble straight through the zone and finish on goal. No passing in the attacking zone. As soon as the attackers break into the attacking zone two players from that end line attack the middle zone going the opposite direction. The ball loser becomes the new defender. Play 20 minutes.

Progression:
If the defender wins the ball counterattack the opposite goal. Play 20 minutes.

Progression:
When the two attackers cross the middle zone and reach the attacking zone a second defender steps off the end line to play against the two. The first defender may chase out of the middle zone. If a defender wins the ball the game goes 2v2 until the ball goes off the field or is shot. Restart the game with a new first defender. Have extra defenders near the half line ready to step in. Play 20 minutes.

Set up:
        Players: 12 players, 2 goalkeepers
        Gear: 4 cones, 7 vests(5+2), 2 goals
        Field: 50 yds long by 44 wide
        Time: 20 minutes

Instructions:
The game is 5v5 plus 2 neutral players who are always on the attacking team. Prior going to goal a 1-2 combination must be played. If a team plays a 1-2 and losses the ball then regains it before the other team plays 3 passes they may go directly back to goal.

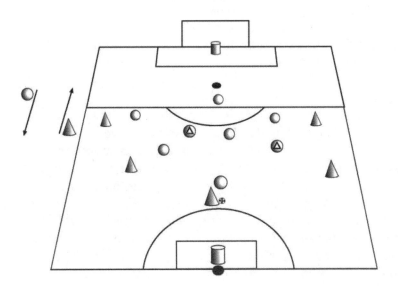

Attacking 2v2 with the Dribble

Objective:
>Technical: Close control dribble.
>Tactical: When to take defender on.

Teaching Points:
>1. Make first touch in attacking direction.
>2. Correct decision to pass or dribble.
>3. Look over the defender's shoulder.

Set up:
>Players: 12
>Gear: 6 vests, 4 cones,12 balls
>Field: 50 x 40 feet
>Time: 20 minutes

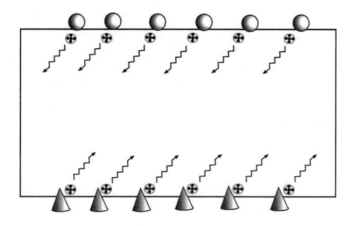

Instructions:
Each player has a ball. Six players are in vests. The two teams face each other across the long sides of the rectangle. On a signal the players dribble across the field then do a turn on the opposite line. Players wait for the next signal to begin again. Vary the moves performed crossing the field. Be certain both teams dribble at each other and perform the required move in the same direction (right or left). Vary the type of turn done at each line.

Set up:

Players: 12
Gear: 6 vests, 4 cones, spare balls
Field: 50 x 40 feet
Time: 40 minutes

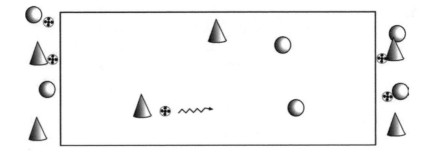

Instructions:

The game is 2v2 on the field. There are also two players from each team on each end line. Two attackers run at two defenders on the field. The objective is to dribble over the end line and do a turn. As soon as this is done, two teammates from the scoring team attack the defenders in the middle in the opposite direction. The two defenders stay in the middle until they win a ball and counter-dribble off the correct end of the field. Games are to 20 points. Play 20 minutes.

Progression:

The two attacking players must now play a 1-2 combination with a teammate on either end line prior to attacking the opposite end line with the dribble. Games are to 20 points. Play 20 minutes.

Set up:

Players: 6v6 with 2 goalkeepers
Gear: 6 vests, 8 cones, 2 goals, spare balls
Field: 60 yards(20-20-20) x 30 Yards
Time: 30 minutes

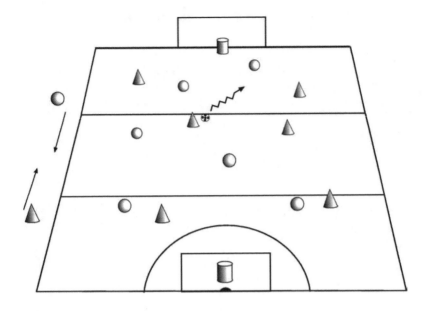

Instructions:
The field is divided into equal thirds and has a 2v2 in each area.
Players must stay in their own third of the field unless they dribble
the ball into the next third for a 3v2. On a lost ball the team must
balance back to 2 players in each third. Play six 5-minute games.
Settle a 3-3 tie with penalty kicks.

Attacking 2v2 with the Pass

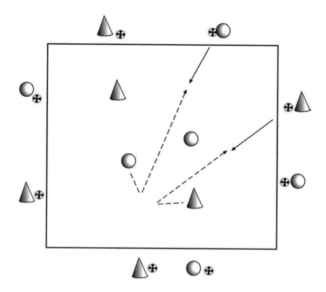

Objective:
>   Technical: Receiving first touch played forward.
>   Tactical: Play an early pass forward to feet.

Teaching points:
>   1. Strike a pass on the ground with correct pace.
>   2. Look forward early to determine options.
>   3. Change direction during runs for the ball.

Set up:
>   Players: 12
>   Gear: 6 vests, 4 cones, 8 balls
>   Field: 40 x 40 feet
>   Time: 60 minutes

Instructions:
There are two players from each team inside the field. The other four
teammates position themselves on the edge of each side of the field
with a ball each. The two middle players make runs toward their
own side teammates and play a 1-2 combination with them. Every
run to find a pass must include a change of direction prior to receiving. Switch middle players every minute. Play 10 minutes.

Progression:
Play with two balls per team which begin with the middle players.
When a pass is made to a teammate on the side that player steps
into the field to play and the original passer takes that side position.
The player coming on the field must change direction with the drib-
ble before passing to another side teammate. Play 10 minutes.

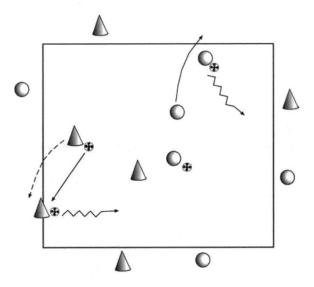

Progression:
Play 2v2 live in the middle with one ball. Side players do not defend
each other. Each game is to 20 successful switches. Play 20 minutes.

Progression:
Same starting positions. To begin play one team plays horizontally
across the field to either of their end line players (east/west). The
other team plays vertically to their end line players (north/south). If
either team chooses to change the direction of play (east/west team
passes to teammate on north/south line) both teams change their
attacking direction. The direction change pass does not count as a
point. 20 successful switches wins the game. Play 20 minutes.

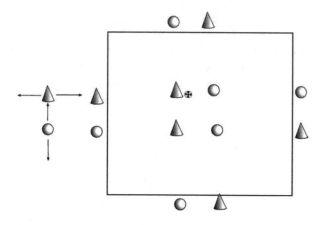

Set up:

Players: 12 with 2 goalkeepers
Gear: 6 vests, 10 cones, 2 goals, spare balls
Field: 60 yards (25-10-25) x width of box
Time: 30 minutes

Instructions:

6v6. Prior to scoring a goal a pass must be played from the defensive side of the field, through the middle zone to the attacking side of the field. If a team loses the ball in the attacking side and regains it, they attempt to finish quickly. If a player gets the ball in the middle zone, it must be dribbled into the attacking side. Play three 10 minute games.

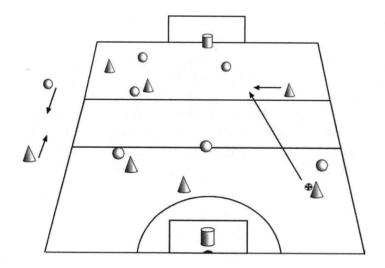

Transition 2v2 Near Goal

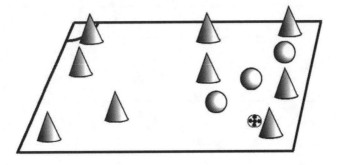

Objective:
       Technical: Low shots in the corners
       Tactical: Move to the correct position on transition.

Teaching points:
       1. Hit the low corner target.
       2. Speed of reaction to transition cue.
       3. Verbal communication when going to defend.

Set up:
       Players: 12
       Gear: 4 cones, 3 vests
       Field: 18 yds x 15 yds
       Time: 10 minutes

Instructions:
The game is 9v3 keep away. The three defenders hold the vests in their hands. When a defender touches the ball the vest is dropped to the ground and the last player to touch the ball picks up the vest and becomes a defender.

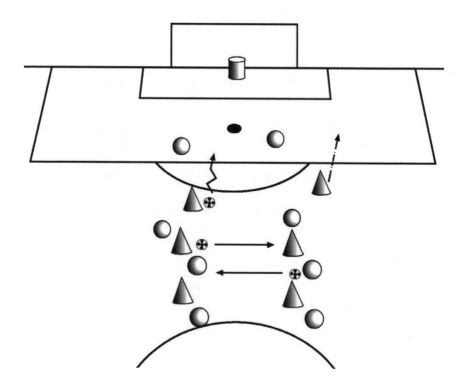

Set up:

      Players: 2 teams of 6 players, 1 GK
      Gear: 2 cones, 6 vests, 1 goal
      Field: 18 yard box by 25 yards
      Time: 60 minutes

Instructions:

The game is 2v2 in front of goal. The attacking pair runs at the defending pair from the top. After the shot the defending pair goes off and the attacking pair defends and a new pair attack. If defenders win they pass to the next pair in line. The pairs in line pass one touch while waiting their turn to attack. Alternate the pairs in line by team. Play 4 games of 5 minutes each. The team with the most goals at time gets one point. The repetitions must be performed at high speed.

Progression:

After the attacking pair has shot on the goal, they defend a serve sent in from the flank against the pair of defenders they've just played who are now attackers. If the defenders stop the original attack and play to the top line, they become attackers and attempt to score off the ball served from width. The original defending pair goes out to serve after the sequence ends. Alternate the serve from side to side. Play 4 games of 5 minutes each.

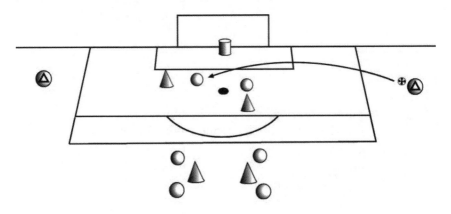

Progression:

The attacking pair has the option to attack the goal directly or play wide to either flank player for an early serve. After the serve the defending pair become attackers and attempt to score from a serve from the opposite flank. If the original attackers go directly to goal without the serve the original defenders attack a wide serve then become defenders again against a serve from the opposite flank. Play 4 games of 5 minutes each.

Set up:

Players: 12 players, 2 GK's
Gear: 4 cones, 6 vests, spare balls
Field: 50 yds by 44 yds
Time: 20 minutes

Instructions:

The game is 6x6. Play 4 games of 5 minutes each. If it ends in a tie go to penalty kicks to decide winner.

Teaching the Diagonal Run 2v2

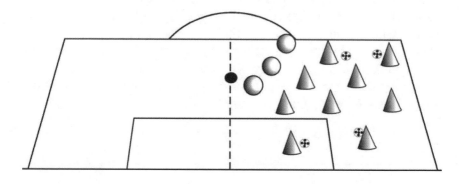

Objective:

Technical: Correct speed & angle of pass.
Tactical: Look to run diagonally behind defenders.

Teaching points:

1. Go at the defending pair at speed.
2. Make diagonal runs behind a defender.
3. Play the pass at the correct time.

Set up:

Players: 12 players
Gear: 4 cones, 3 vests, 5 balls
Field: Half the penalty box
Time: 10 minutes

Instructions:

The game is tag. There are three "it" players holding vests in their
hands and nine players running. When tagged a player takes the
vest and becomes an "it" player. A player is safe when possessing
one of the four balls being played about the field. Play 10 minutes.

Set up:

Players: 12 players
Gear: 10 cones, 4 vests, 2 goals, spare balls
Field: 36 yds x 20 yds with halfway line
Time: 80 minutes

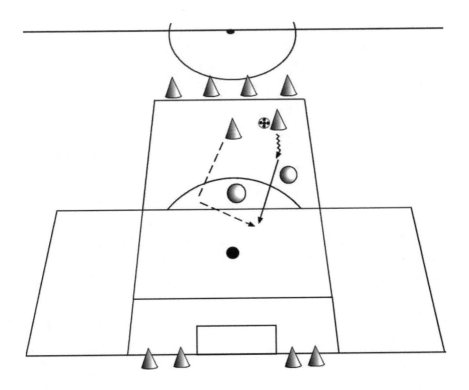

Instructions:

The game is 2v2. Two attackers begin on one end line with a ball. The two defenders begin in that half of the field. The attackers attempt to beat them then dribble off the opposite end line using a diagonal run. The two defenders can not chase over the line. If the defenders win the ball they counter attack and dribble off the correct end line. The pair losing the ball becomes defenders. The halfway line is an offside line. If caught offside that pair become defenders. Play 20 minutes.

Progression:

Add a small cone goal at each corner of each end line. When the two defenders are beaten, two new defenders step onto the field off the opposite end line. If they win the ball they counter toward the two defenders in the middle then attempt to attack a cone goal on the opposite end line against another defending pair. A point is scored when a cone goal is passed through. Play 4 games of 5 minutes each.

Progression:
Add the two full goals and the goalkeepers. The second pair of defenders is now positioned on the field behind the middle two defenders. Play 4 games of 5 minutes each. The partners compete against each other.

Progression:
There are three teams of four players each playing the width of the box.. The game is 4v4. The team that scores the goal stays on and the losing team switches with the resting team quickly. Play is resumed after a goal by the team coming on starting with the ball from the end of the field opposite from where the goal was scored from. The halfway line is an offside line. Defenders must play in front of the line until the ball goes in. Play 2 games of 10 minutes each.

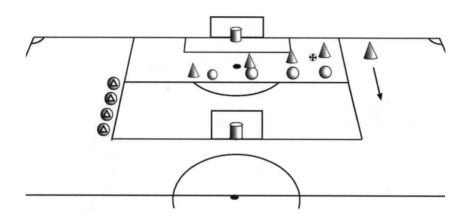

Finishing 2v2

Objective:
Technical: Finishing a served ball quickly.
Tactical: Correct timing of near/far post runs.

Teaching Points:
1. Drive the serve head high from the flank.
2. Accelerate to goal when the server commits.
3. Shoot first time whenever possible.

Set up:
Players: 12 players. 2 Goalkeepers
Gear: 6 cones, 8 vests (2 colors), 2 goals, balls
Field: 36 yds x 44 yds
Time: 90 minutes

Instructions:
There are three teams of four players each. Two of the teams pass through the air to each other side to side across the width of the field using four balls. The third team moves freely between the groups playing 1-2 combinations with the wide players setting up their serve to the opposite side. Keepers stay in the middle of the field and attempt to cut serves off using their hands. Switch a new team into the middle every 2 minutes. Play 10 minutes.

Progression:
The game is 2v2 in each half plus 4 neutral players wide. Players in the 2v2's may not cross the halfway line. They may use the neutrals, who choose to play a direct serve back in the same half or a diagonal serve to the opposite half's 2v2. Play 2 minute games then switch the wide team in. Play 30 minutes. (see diagram)

Progression:
Remove the halfway line and play 6v6 with two players from each team playing as wide servers. Play 4 games of 5 minutes each. Rotate the wide players.

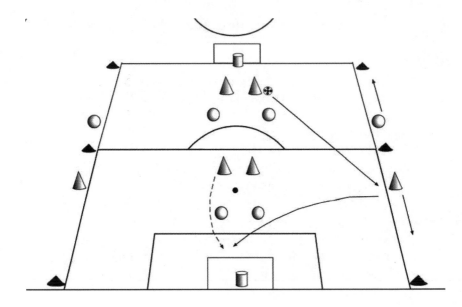

Progression:
Move one goal to the center circle and play 6v6. Play games to five.
Play 30 minutes.

Progression:
A first touch goal counts as 2 points.

Progression:
A first touch goal from a first touch pass is 3 points.

Transition to Attack with an Early Pass

Objective:

> Technical: Striking low accurate passes forward.
> Tactical: Looking up-field early for target players.

Teaching Points:

> 1. Drive the pass with power.
> 2. Play forward quickly on a won ball.
> 3. Move forward to support the pass.

Set up:

> Players: 12 players, 2 Goalkeepers
> Gear: 8 cones, 8 vests (2 colors), 2 goals, balls
> Field: 36 yds x 44 yds
> Time: 90 minutes

Instructions:

There are three teams of four players each. Each team has a ball. The first movement is passing to each other in 1-2-3-4 number sequence. Each player is assigned a number. The second movement is passing in any sequence using two touches. The third movement is playing one touch without playing to your own team. Play 20 minutes.

Progression:

The game is 4v4 with the third team positioned one between the goal post and the corner on each end line playing as neutrals. There is a keeper in each goal. The objective is to play a pass from the defensive half to a neutral player or goalkeeper on the opposite end line. If the team making the pass all move to the new half and keep the ball they score one point. All players must always move to the half the ball is in. The neutrals and goalkeepers may help the teams keep possession. Play 6 games of 5 minutes each. Rotate the teams each game. *(see diagram on following page)*

Progression:

The game is now to goal. After receiving the driven pass the neutrals now pass back to an advancing attacking player who may go directly to goal or pass to a teammate. For the goal to count all attacking

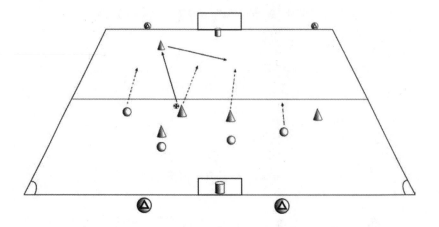

players must be in the attacking half. Play 4 games of 5 minutes each. Rotate the teams each game.

Progression:
The game is now 6v6. A goal scored as a result of a pass over the half line counts as two goals. Play 4 games of 5 minutes each. Settle a 2-2 tie with matching penalty kicks.

Transition with an Early Pass Forward

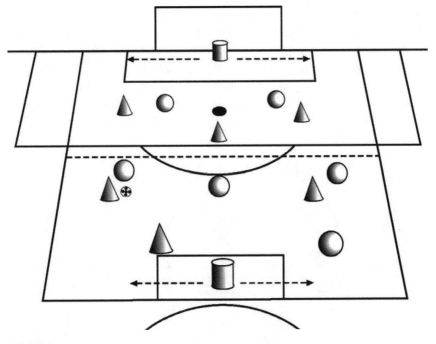

Objective:
>Technical: Striking a driven ball to feet.
>Tactical: Recognition of the moment to pass forward.

Teaching Points:
>1. Rapid conversion to attack mode on a won ball.
>2. Checking striker's position as the ball is won.
>3. Early pass to feet or to attacking space.

Set up:
>Players: 12 players, 2 goalkeepers
>Gear: 10 cones, 6 vests, 2 goals, balls
>Field: 40 yds by 30 yds with a halfway line
>Time: 90 minutes

Instructions:
The two teams play 6v6. A goalkeeper is positioned on each end line. A team scores a point when they pass over the half line to a goalkeeper then get the ball back. The games are to 10. Play 20 minutes.

Progression:
The game is 4v4 to goal. There are 2 neutral players for each team positioned between the goal post and corner of the field near the goal they are attacking. A pass must be played from the one half to a target player who gets two touches to play the ball back in to a teammate for a shot. If a team loses then wins a ball in the attacking half they may go directly to goal or use an end line player. Teams may shoot at either goal. Play 4 games of 5 minutes each.

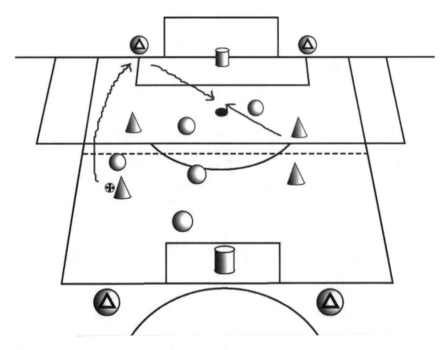

Progression:
The teams now play toward a specified goal. Both teams have 2 target players on an end line who are switched after goals. Play 4 games of 5 minutes each.

Progression:
The teams play 6v6 all over the field. The half line must be passed over. The ball may not be dribbled over the half line. Play 2 games of 10 minutes each.

Playing the Pass Up the Field

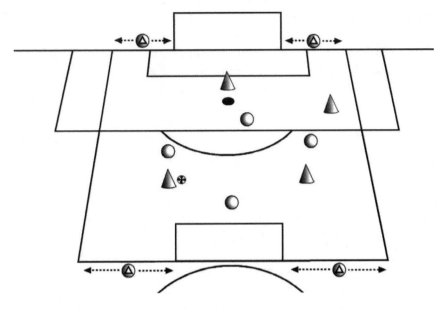

Objective:

    Technical: Accurate medium/long passes.
    Tactical: See the target player's intentions.

Teaching points:

    1. Make eye contact with the target player.
    2. Play forward as the first choice pass.
    3. Quick feet moving to support end line players.

Set up:

    Players: 12 players
    Gear: 4 cones, 12 vests, (2 colors), balls
    Field: 44 yds by 30 yds
    Time: 90 minutes

Instructions:

There are 3 teams of 4 players each. The players on each team are numbered 1 2 3 4. Each team passes a ball in numerical order while moving. Change to even numbers passing to odd numbers. Change to a two touch game. Lastly, combine the three teams and play a one touch game using 4 balls. Play 20 minutes.

Progression:

Play 4v4 possession inside the field. The third team is positioned two each on each end line and play neutral. When a team plays a 1-2 with an end line player they score one point. The end line player's first touch must be into the field. Play games to 10 points. Switch teams quickly after each game. Play 20 minutes.

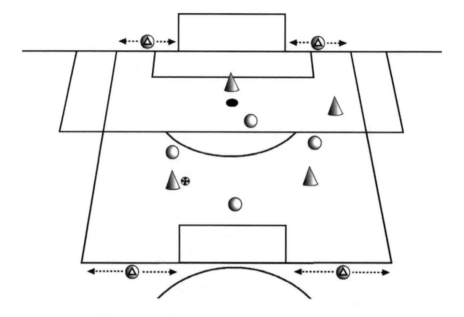

Progression:

Teams must play to both end lines in the same possession for the point to count. The winning team stays on. Play 20 minutes.

Progression:

Add a goal and a goalkeeper to each end line. The field players must pass to an end line player prior to going to goal. The end line player gets two touches. If a team loses the ball after playing to an end line player then regain it prior to the opponents doing so they may go directly back to goal. Play 6 games of 5 minutes each.

Playing the Split Pass Up the Field

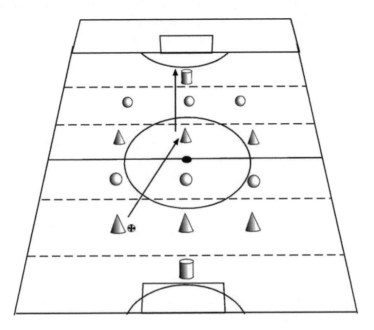

Objective:

>   Technical: Striking a pass forward between two defenders.
>   Tactical: Receiver shows the split to the passer.

Teaching Points:

>   1. Play a quick square pass if no split is available.
>   2. Receiver splits defenders and positions side on.
>   3. See receiver between defenders & pass to feet.

Set up:

>   Players: 12 players, 2 goalkeepers
>   Gear: 10 cones, 6 vests, 2 goals, spare balls
>   Field: 70 x 44 yds (4 zones of 10 yds/2 15 yd end zones)
>   Time: 90 minutes

Instructions:

The game is 6v6. There are three players from each team in each alternating zone. The goalkeepers play in front of each goal. The objective is for either team to pass from one of their zones through an opponent's zone to a teammate in the next zone. The team then attempts to play to the goalkeeper who distributes to the team in the zone directly in front of the goal and the game direction is changed. The pass from zone to zone must be a split pass. Defenders must react fairly to lateral ball movement. The game is continuous end to end. Play 20 minutes.

Progression:
The game is now directional and to goal. To score, the ball must be a split pass from the defensive zone to the attacking zone in front of goal. The receiver must shoot within three touches. Play restarts with the opposition in their defensive zone attempting to pass forward to the attacking zone. If the defenders cut the pass off they look quickly to play a split pass forward to a teammate who goes to goal. Play 2 games of 10 minutes each.

Progression:
When a defender cuts off a pass, he either plays an early split pass forward or attacks the next zone on the dribble. If the player dribbles forward to the next zone the player who made the original bad pass must defend the attacking player 1v1. Play 2 games of 10 minutes each.

Progression:
The two teams play 6v6, both utilizing a flat 3-3 system. If a goal is scored as a result of a split pass it counts as 2 points. Play 2 games of 15 minutes each.

Creating Attack From the Center

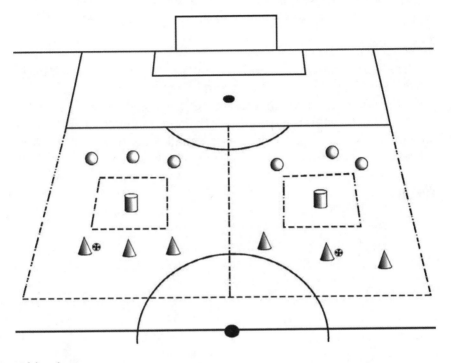

Objectives:
Technical: Accurate passing to a central target player.
Tactical: Play away from then toward the target area.

Teaching points:
1. Target player assumes side-on position to ball.
2. The pass is played to the target player's lead foot.
3. Don't crowd the target area.

Set up:
Players: 12 players, 2 goalkeepers
Gear:　16 cones, 6 vests, spare balls
Field:　30 yds x 25 yds with a box in middle. (2fields)
Time:　30 minutes

Instructions:
There are six players and one goalkeeper who plays with hands on
each field. The game is 3v3 possession with the neutral goalkeeper

positioned inside the small box in the center. When either team plays to the goalkeeper and receives the ball back they get one point. Play 3 games of 5 minutes each.

Progression:
Each team now defends an end line. To score a point the ball must be dribbled over the opposition's end line after receiving a pass from the goalkeeper, who now uses feet only. After getting a pass from the goalkeeper, if the attacking team loses then regains the ball before the opposition plays to the goalkeeper they may attack the end line directly. Play 3 games of 5 minutes each.

Set up:
Players: 12 players, 2 goalkeepers
Gear: 8 cones, 6 vests, spare balls
Field: half field with a box in middle
Time: 60 minutes

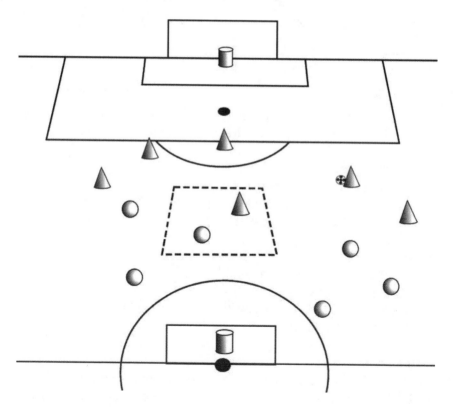

Instructions:

The game is 6v6 to goal. The players are positioned 5v5 on the field and one player from each team is positioned in the small box. These two players do not compete with each other. The ball must be passed to the team's target player in the small box prior to going to goal. The target player has the option to either dribble out of the box to attack or pass to a teammate and join the attack. A teammate takes the previous target player's position inside the box. If the ball is then lost and regained prior to the opposition using their target player, they may go back directly to goal. Play 4 games of 5 minutes each.

Progression:

The two players in the middle box now compete 1v1 against each other. Other field players may not double team the target players in the small box. Play 4 games of 5 minutes each.

Progression:

The middle box is left open. Players must check into the box to receive a pass then attack the goal. They must not loiter inside the box if they don't get a pass. Play 2 games of 10 minutes each.

Attacking Wide Out of Midfield

Objective:
Technical: Correct speed and angle of pass to width.
Tactical: Safe possession looking to play wide.

Teaching Points:
1. Play a diagonal pass for the wide player
2. Keep body position open to the width.
3. Lead the wide player with the pass.

Set up:
Players: 12 players, 2 Goalkeepers
Gear: 6 vests, 8 cones, 2 goals, balls
Field: 50 yds x 44 yds
Time: 90 minutes

Instructions:
The game is 6v6 keep away. The keepers move freely around the field and are neutral. They play using their hands. Play 10 minutes.

Progression: (see diagram on following page)
There is a 4v4 on the field. There are also two players from each team positioned wide just outside the touchline near the midfield line. After a team completes three consecutive passes in its own half they play a diagonal pass which leads the wide player who moves forward at speed, controls the ball, then serves the team-mates who have made runs forward to goal. If the team regains the ball after an unsuccessful scoring move before the opposition makes three passes, they may attack the goal directly. Rotate the wide players. Play three games of ten minutes each.

Progression:
The players positioned wide play live 1v1. The pair of wide players on the weak side go forward to participate in the movement by covering the back post. Play two games of ten minutes each.

Progression:
The game is 6v6 using the entire width of the field. A goal from a wide serve counts two. A goal from play is one point. Play three games of ten minutes each.

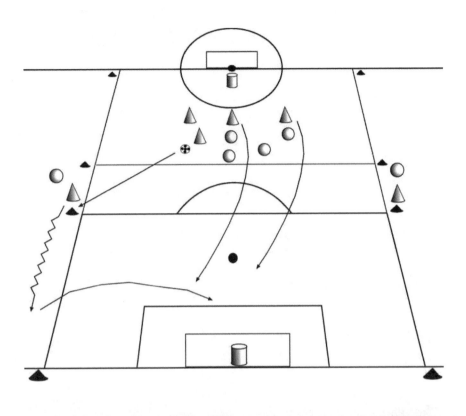

Combination Play to Get Forward

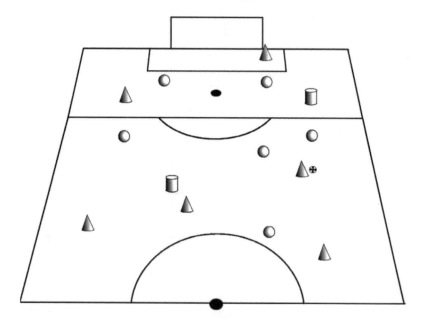

Objective:

    Technical: First time passing to moving players.

    Tactical: Determination to get forward toward goal.

Teaching Points:

    1. Look to play forward to feet early.

    2. Layoff players must show to the ball.

    3. The runs forward must be aggressive.

Set up:

    Players: 12 players, 2 goalkeepers

    Gear: 8 cones, 6 vests, 2 goals, balls

    Field: 50 yds by 44. 10 yd middle zone

    Time: 90 minutes

Instructions:

The game is 6v6 keep away. The goalkeepers are neutral and move freely around the field. Vary the distribution of the goalkeepers to the players. Play 20 minutes.

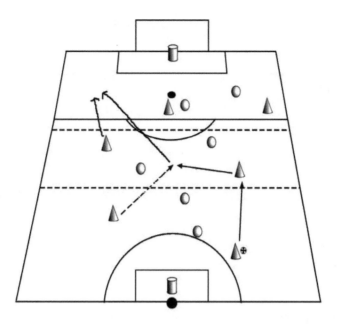

Progression:
The game is 6v6 to goal. Two players from each team must remain in the middle zone and act as target players for combination play coming from the back. Target players may not be defended. The other eight players move freely around the field. When a team begins an attack from its defensive zone one of the two target players must be used. The original passer or a teammate must get the pass from the target player then the goal is attacked. Switch the target players on the fly. Play 20 minutes.

Progression:
When a team begins an attack from its own defensive zone the pass must be played all the way through the middle zone to a player in the attacking half. A player moving forward from the middle zone must get the next pass then attack the goal. New player becomes target in middle zone. Play 3 games of 10 minutes each.

Progression:
Play 6v6. If an attack begins in a teams defensive zone and the middle zone is passed all the way through, the goal counts double. Play 2 games of 10 minutes each.

Turning to Attack

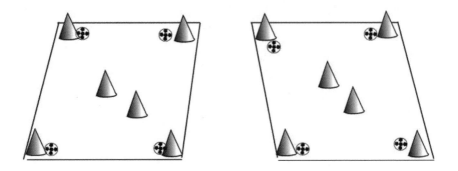

Objective:
> Technical: Turning after moving toward the ball.
> Tactical: Look over the shoulder to check the defender.

Teaching Points:
> 1. Make eye contact with and move toward the passer.
> 2. Choose the turn while moving toward the passer.
> 3. Make shoulder or hip feint before each turn.

Set up:
> Players: 12 players
> Gear: 8 cones, 6 vests, balls
> Field: 20 yds by 20 yds. (2 fields)
> Time: 20 minutes

Instructions:
There are two teams of six players each. All four side players have a ball. Two players are positioned inside the field. The players in the middle get a pass from a side player. Upon receiving the ball the middle player will do a turn away then a turn back towards the side player (two turns). The middle player then passes to the side player and the two switch positions. Play 10 minutes.

Progression:

The two middle players have a ball each. They play a 1-2 then turn and play to an open side player. They then switch positions. Play 10 minutes.

Set up:

Players: 12 players
Gear: 4 cones, 8 vests (2 colors), balls
Field: 44 yds by 25 yds
Time: 40 minutes

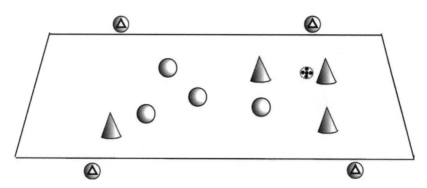

Instructions:

There are three teams of four players each. Two of the teams play 4v4 possession on the field. The third team is positioned near the corners of the field on the two long sides and are neutral. A point is scored when a player completes a successful turn off a pass from a teammate or a neutral player on the corner. Play games to 10 successful turns. Defenders must play tight. Alternate teams. Play 20 minutes.

Progression:

The neutral players are now positioned two each on the end lines of the field. The field player receiving the pass must perform a turn and attack the opposite end line. Play 20 minutes.

Set up:

      Players: 12 players, 2 goalkeepers
      Gear: 8 cones, 6 vests, 2 goals, balls
      Field: 50 yds by 44 yds
      Time: 30 minutes

Instructions:

The game is 6v6 to goal. If a player turns with the ball and beats a defender to create an attack it counts as 1 point. Goals count for 2 points. Play games to 5 points.

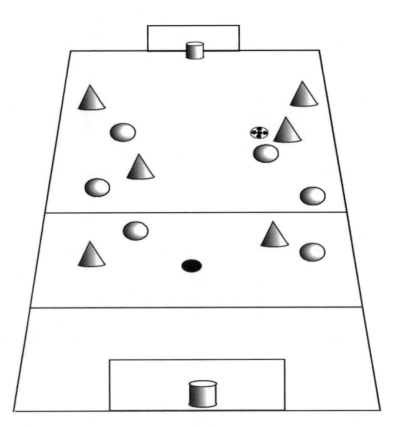

Receiving Side-on to Attack

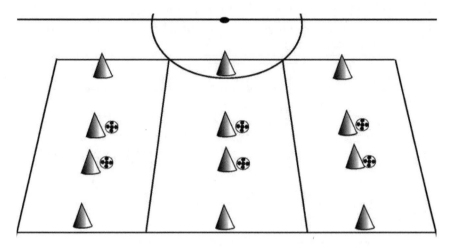

Objective:
>Technical: Inside foot receiving, second touch forward.
>Tactical: Keep eyes up and looking forward to attack.

Teaching points:
>1. Play firm passes to players checking back.
>2. Lift eyes to look up the field on the first touch.
>3. Push second touch up the field and attack.

Set up:
>Players: 12 players
>Gear: 6 cones, 6 balls
>Field: 30 yds x width of penalty area
>Time: 30 minutes

Instructions:
There are three groups of four players each playing on three fields. A field is two cones placed 30 yards apart. Provide ample room between fields. There are two balls per field. To begin there is a player near each endline and two players working in the middle. The middle players move to each end player with a ball then play a 1-2 combination. They receive side on with the inside foot, use opposite foot for the second touch then dribble toward the opposite end and play another 1-2. Switch the pairs after playing 1 minute. Play 15 minutes.

Progression:
After receiving with the inside foot the second touch must be played with the outside of the same foot. The third touch should be a pass forward. Play 15 minutes.

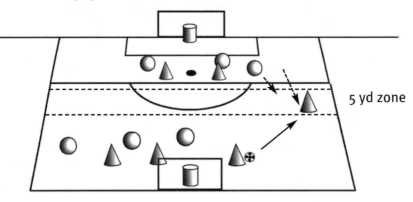

5 yd zone

Set up:
Players: 12 players, 2 Goalkeepers
Gear: 8 cones, 6 vests, 2 goals, Balls
Field: 40 yds x 30 yds with 5 yd middle zone
Time: 60 minutes

Instructions:
There is a 3v3 in each end of the field. The middle zone begins free. Prior to going to goal a team must pass to a teammate who has checked back into the middle zone to receive the pass side on. The defenders are not live until the ball is passed or dribbled forward into the attacking zone for a 3v3. If the ball is lost then won back they go directly back to goal. After a goal the scorers get the ball back and the attacking direction changes. Play four games of five minutes each.

Progression:
The defenders are live immediately after the checking back player has received the pass in the middle zone. Play four games of five minutes each.

Progression:
The entire middle zone is now live for the defenders. They may enter only when an attacker goes in. Play two games of ten minutes each.

Counterattacking with the Speed Dribble

Objective:
>   Technical: Speed dribbling to beat an opponent.
>   Tactical: Bursting forward with the ball with eyes up.

Teaching Points:
>   1. Play the first touch forward and burst onto it.
>   2. Identify when to accelerate past a defender.
>   3. Keep eyes moving when dribbling in space.

Set up:
>   Players: 12 players
>   Gear: 8 cones, 6 vests, 6 balls
>   Field: 50 yds x 44 yds with 15 yd middle zone
>   Time: 30 minutes

Instructions:
There are two teams moving freely around the field. One team begins with a ball each. They dribble at any opponent who plays only passive defense. After sprinting past the defender the player with the ball recovers to a jogging dribble then begins a run at a different defender. Teams play 1 minute then switch roles. Play 10 min.

Progression:
The six defenders now begin in the middle zone. The opposite six players with the balls play a 1-2 with a defender and run past that passive defender with the speed dribble to the opposite end of the field. Teams play 1 minute then switch roles. Play 10 minutes.

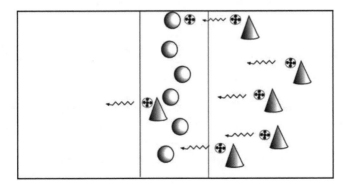

Progression:
The defenders in the middle zone are now live but may not chase attackers out. When an attacker gets through the zone it is one point for the team. If a defender wins the ball from an attacker the opposite endline is counter- attacked for 2 points. After five attacks, the opposite team gets five attacks. The team with the most total points wins the game. Play 10 minutes.

Set up:
       Players: 12 players, 2 goalkeepers
       Gear: 8 cones, 8 vests (2 colors), 2 goals
       Field: 50yds x 44 yds with 15 yard middle zone
       Time: 60 minutes

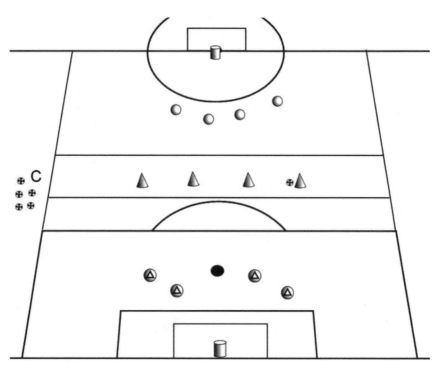

Instructions:
There are three teams of four players each playing to goal. Begin with a team in each end and a team in the middle zone who has the ball. The middle zone team attacks one of the teams defending a goal. If they score they get one point. They then turn and attack the

defenders on the opposite end. If the defenders win the ball the movement is over. The goalkeeper rolls a new ball to the attackers and they attack the opposite end at speed. Switch the attacking team after two minutes. Play 10 minutes.

Progression:
If the defenders win the ball they can counterattack the team positioned in the opposite end. The team that lost the ball can not chase the ball into the middle zone. The middle zone is free and is used to organize the counterattack. Play 2 games of 10 minutes each.

Progression:
The game is now 6v6. The middle zone must be dribbled through if the ball is won in the defending half of the field. Play 2 games of 10 minutes each.

Attacking Possession 7v5

Objective:
>Technical: Playing two and three touch.
>Tactical: Getting extra players into attacking positions.

Teaching Points:
>1. Receiving touch is away from the body.
>2. Head up looking for moving teammates.
>3. Players' runs are communication to the passer.

Set up:
>Players: 12 players, 2 Goalkeepers
>Gear: 4 cones, 8 vests (2 colors),2 goals,balls
>Field: Half field by 44 yds wide
>Time: 90 minutes

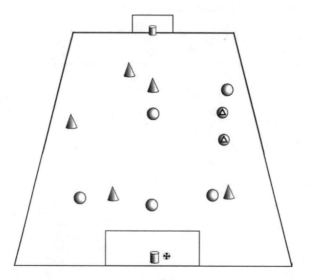

Instructions:
The game is 5v5 with 2 neutral players identified by their vest color.
They both play with the team in possession. The keepers are in goal.
When a team plays to either keeper and gets the ball back they score
one point. The keepers use their feet. Play games to 10 points. Play
10 minutes.

Progression:

The teams must play to both keepers during the same possession for the point to count. Keepers kick out bouncing balls into play. Play games to 10 points. Play 10 minutes.

Progression:

The game is now live to goal. The teams play three touch while the two neutral players get two touches. The exception is when a player decides to attack the goal on the dribble or has used all three touches and must dribble to goal. Play 10 minutes.

Progression:

All players have unlimited touches on the ball. The two neutral players stay on a specific team until the opposition scores a goal. The two neutrals will then switch over to that team and the game continues. Play 2 games of 10 minutes each.

Progression:

The two neutral players will now also switch teams when the team of five completes five consecutive passes in the same possession. Play 2 games of 10 minutes each.

Progression:

Play 6v6. The emphasis is to choose an early pass to a teammate. Use the dribble if it will create a scoring chance. Play 2 games of 10 minutes each.

Possession 6v6

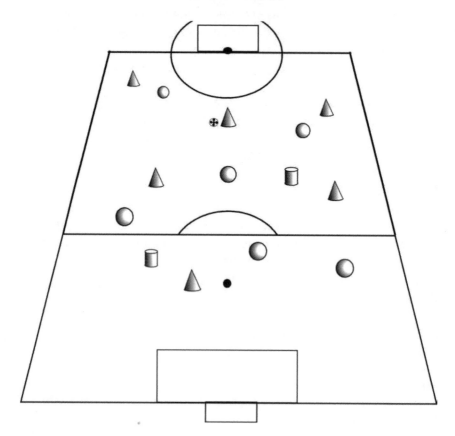

Objective:

    Technical: Improve Passing & receiving.

    Tactical: Increase Mobility & Vision.

Teaching Points:

    1. Pass and receive the ball with the correct foot.

    2. Make the receiving touch away from pressure.

    3. Movement & communication off the ball.

Set up:

    Players: 12 players, 2 goalkeepers

    Gear: 6 vests, 4 cones, 2 goals, spare balls

    Field: 50yds x 44 yds

    Time: 90 minutes

Instructions:

The two teams play keep away. A point is scored when a pass is played to either neutral goalkeeper and received back by the team. The goalkeepers are allowed to move freely and use their hands. Vary the types of service to the goalkeepers as well as their distribution to the field players. Play three 5 minute games.

Progression:

The game is now to goal. The defending team is allowed to play as six "field goalkeepers" to win the ball. The ball winner may drop the ball if caught and dribble, pass or may also throw the ball to a teammate. The opposite team now plays as field goalkeepers. Play three 5 minute games.

Progression:

There are three games. Play 2 halves of 10 minutes each per game.

Game 1. After scoring, the team must complete six consecutive passes before going back to goal.

Game 2. Teams may not play the same type of pass (forward, square, back) twice in a row.

Game 3. Teams must pass in the direction they face when receiving a pass or choose to dribble in that direction.

Possession in Tight Space

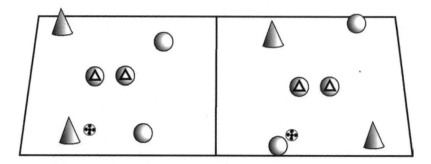

Objectives:
Technical: Short passes played to feet.
Tactical: Rapid movement into supporting positions.

Teaching Points:
1. Play quick side footed passes.
2. Move the ball quickly away from where it was received.
3. Move to give close angle support to the ball.

Set up:
Players: 12 players
Gear: 8 cones, 8 vests (2 colors), spare balls
Field: 40 ft by 20 ft with halfway line (2 fields)
Time: 60 minutes

Instructions:
The game is 4v2 possession on each field. There are two players of each shirt color on the field. Two players begin as defenders. When they win the ball they immediately   become attackers while the pair that lost the ball becomes defenders. Play 10 games of 2 minutes each. The pair on defense at time begin as defenders in the next game.

Progression:
There is again a 4v2 in each half. The game is two touch using only one ball. Players must stay in their own half. The game begins with one pair as defenders in each half. The two teams in possession may pass across the halfway line to each other. When a defending pair wins the ball, their partners join them on the half the ball was won

on and the ball losing team become defenders in each half. Play 10 games of 2 minutes each. The team on defense at time begins the next game as defenders and must win the ball twice to get out.

Progression:
The game is 2v2v2. There is a team of two in each half and the third team begins on an end line with a ball. The objective of the two on the end line is to beat both defensive pairs and get the ball over the opposite end line under control. Defensive pairs must remain in their own half. If the defensive pair wins the ball they counterattack the opposite end line. The pair that lost the ball can not chase out of the half they lost the ball in. Teams get one point for each end line crossed. Play 4 games of 5 minutes each.

Set up:
      Players: 12 players, 2 goalkeepers
      Gear: 8 cones, 8 vests,(2 colors) 2 goals
      Field: 50 yds by 30 yds in thirds
      Time: 30 minutes

Instructions:
The game is 4v4v4 to goal. There is one team in each third of the field. The team in the middle begins by attacking one of the goals. If they score they turn around and attack the opposite goal. If the defenders win, they counterattack the opposite goal. The middle zone is safe. Defending players may not chase into the middle. Play 3 games of 10 minutes each.

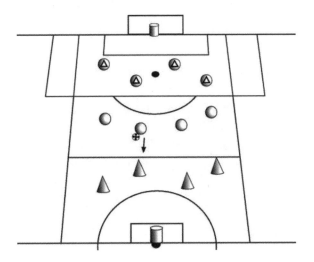

Possession Playing to Target Players

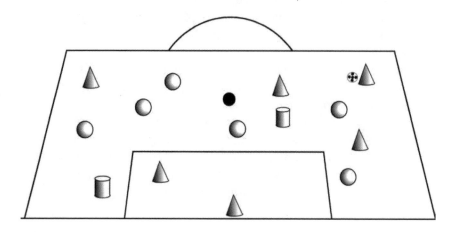

Objectives:
Technical: Receiving with the correct foot.
Tactical: When moving without the ball, see the target players.

Teaching Points:
1. Play first touch away from the body.
2. Make the safe pass to feet.
3. Continually look to find position of targets.

Set up:
Players: 12 players, 2 goalkeepers
Gear: 4 cones, 6 vests, spare balls
Field: the 18 yd box
Time: 10 minutes

Instructions:
The game is keep away 6v6 plus two neutral goalkeepers. The ball is passed from player to player by throwing it. If the ball touches the ground or a player is tagged while holding it constitutes a turnover. Five steps maximum. The first pass is free after a turnover.

Set up:

Players: 12 players
Gear: 4 cones, 7 vests (2 colors), spare balls
Field: 44 yds by 30 yds
Time: 40 minutes

Instructions:

The game is 5v5 possession with 2 neutral target players. The target players get 3 touch. When a target player gets a pass and completes the next pass the team in possession gets one point. Play 5 games of 4 minutes each. Change the target players each game.

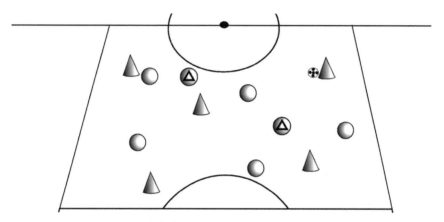

Progression:

The teams get three touches and the target players get two touches. Both target players must be played through in the same possession to score one point. Play 5 games of 4 minutes each.

Set up:

Players: 12 players, 2 goalkeepers
Gear: 4 cones, 7 vests (3 colors), 2 goals, balls
Field: 50 yds by 44 yds
Time: 40 minutes

Instructions:

The game is 6v6 to goal. Each team has a target player in a contrast-ing colored vest. Prior to a team going to goal the ball must go through the target player. If the ball is lost and regained before the opponents make a target pass they may go directly to goal without the target player being used. Play 2 games of 10 minutes each.

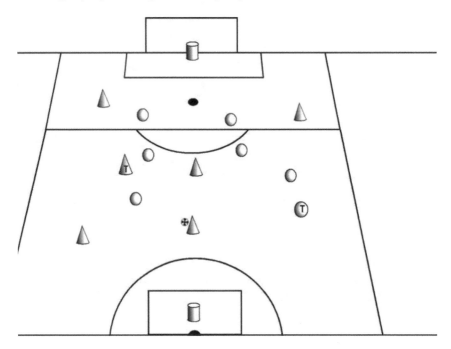

Progression:

The game is 6v6 to goal. The two target players are now regular team players. Play 2 games of 10 minutes each.

Mobility After Receiving a Pass

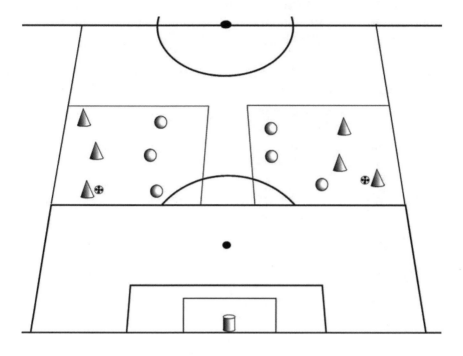

Objectives:

    Technical: Improve passing & receiving.
    Tactical: Moving to new space.

Teaching Points:

    1. Receive a pass, play then move.
    2. Perform feint & accelerate away after receiving.
    3. Speed bursts on running direction changes.

Set up:

    Players: 12
    Gear: 6 vests, 8 cones, spare balls
    Field: 2 fields 15 x 20 yds
    Time: 20 minutes

Instructions:

There are six players per field. The game is always 3v2, three touch keep away. The defending team plays one of their players knee down. When the two teammates win the ball from the three opponents the kneeling player joins in and one player from the ball losing team kneels down. If by the 3rd touch a pass has not been played the player in possession must give the ball up and go knee down. The team with the ball at time gets 1 point. Play 2 minute games.

Set up:

Players: 6v6
Gear: 6 vests, 4 cones, 6 balls
Field: half field
Time: 40 minutes

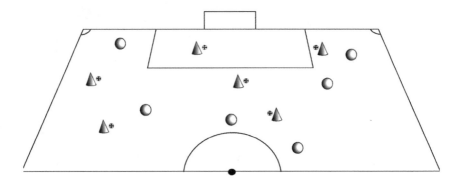

Instructions:
There are 2 teams of 6 players each. All players move freely. One team has a ball for each player. They are the passing team, while the opposite team is the receiving team. The passers get all passes played to them at their feet from the receivers. The receivers are the working team. Passes should be about 20/30 yards. The teams switch roles every 2 minutes.

1st Move:
The receiver checks away at an angle then hard back to the passer, receives the ball, lays the ball off then moves away quickly. The receiver jogs to recover then repeats the move with a different passer.

2nd Move:
After laying the ball off the receiver makes a feint then changes direction and sprints away 5 yards.

3rd Move:
After laying the ball off the receiver sprints away 5 yards backwards.

4th Move:
After collecting a pass the receiver makes a feint then speed dribbles away 10 yards.

Set up:
        Players: 6v6 with 2 Goalkeepers
        Gear: 6 vests, 8 cones, 2 goals, spare balls
        Field: 50 yds x 44 yds
        Time: 30 minutes

Instructions:
There is a 3v3 in each half. The ball must be passed over the halfway line. After the ball has crossed the halfway line one attacking player may step up into the attacking half to create a 4v3 situation. The teams balance back to a 3v3 on a lost ball. After a goal the scoring team gets the ball back and attacks the opposite goal. Play 5 minute games.

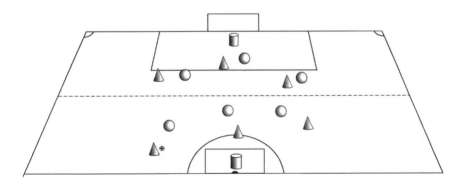

Team Movement After a Penetrating Pass

Objectives:
>Technical: Driven balls played to a runner's feet.
>Tactical: Bend run while moving forward to receive pass.

Teaching Points:
>1. Create possession looking to play long.
>2. Timing and types of runs by target players.
>3. Angles of support runs coming forward.

Set up:
>Players: 12 players, 2 Goalkeepers
>Gear: 8 cones, 6 vests, 2 goals, balls
>Field: 50 yds x 44 yds
>Time: 90 minutes

Instructions:
The game is 6v6. To begin the teams are combined. They move freely over the entire field passing 4-5 balls between them. Players must move continuously. When a goalkeeper calls a player's name that player shoots to the keeper's hands. Play 10 minutes.

Progression:
The game begins 6x6 in one half of the field. The team in possession may use the keeper's feet. The objective is to drive a ball to the keeper on the opposite end of the field and all teammates and defenders must move forward to the new half. The keeper may use feet only. If the keeper is able to distribute the ball to the passing team, they score 1 point. Prior to playing another long pass, all teammates of the passing team must be in the same half of the field. Play 4 games of 5 minutes each.
(see diagram on following page)

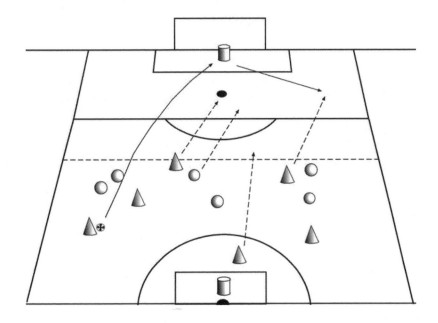

Progression:
The game begins 4v4 in one end of the field. On the opposite end
there is a 2v2. The team with the ball attempts to play a driven pass
to one of its two target players on the opposite end. The receiving
target player must lay the ball off to an attacking player coming forward before the team can go to goal. Two players from each team
must move into the new half for a new 4v4. If the defenders win the
ball they play across to the opposite half, then players move back to
create another 4v4. If the original attacking team loses then wins
the ball back before this pass they can go directly back to goal. Play
4 games of 5 minutes each.

Progression:
The target player may play to the other target player prior to the
team going to goal. All other player movements remain as before.
Play 4 games of 5 minutes each.

Progression:
Play 6v6. Both teams move freely. The ball must be passed through
the middle zone. It may be dribbled through only if there is a loose
ball inside. Play 2 games of 10 minutes each.

Speed of Play

Objectives:
> Technical: Correct receiving touch to set up the pass.
> Tactical: Constant movement adjusting to the ball.

Teaching Points:
> 1. Pass on the ground to the correct foot.
> 2. Play the first touch on an angle into space.
> 3. Adjust support position as it relates to the ball.

Set up:
> Players: 12 Players
> Gear: 4 cones, 12 vests (3 colors), 4 balls
> Field: 36 yds by 44 yds
> Time: 60 minutes

Instructions:
There are 3 teams of 4 players each. They play together with four balls. One team plays two touch while the other 2 teams play unlimited touch. Change the two touch team every 2 minutes. Play 10 minutes.

Progression:
Take away 2 balls. All three teams play one touch.

Progression:
One team of four take positions along each sideline of the field and act as neutral players. The other two teams play 4 v 4 inside the field attempting to keep possession with the help of the neutral players. The neutrals get two touches. The first must be into the

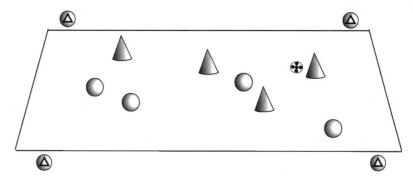

field where they become momentarily live. The games are two minutes long. The team in possession at time gets a point. Play 20 minutes.

Progression:
Three passes must be made inside the field prior to using a neutral player. The neutrals get one touch. If they have to use a second touch the pass must go to another neutral player who then must play first time into the field. Play 20 minutes.

Set up:
       Players: Three teams of four players with two GK's
       Gear: 4 cones, 12 vests (3 colors), 2 goals,
       Field: 36 yds x 44 yds
       Time: 30 minutes

Instructions:
Play games of 4v4. The teams get two touches. If a player takes a third touch that player must go solo to goal or pass to a side player. The resting team is positioned two on each sideline and plays one touch. Keep the game tempo high. Play 5 minute games.

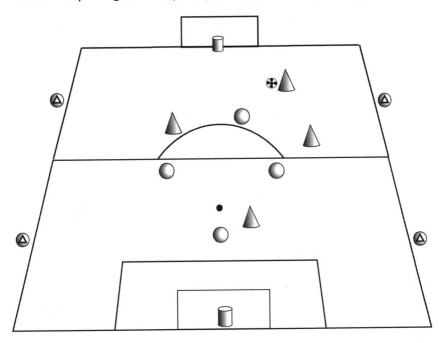

Vision and Concentration During Possession

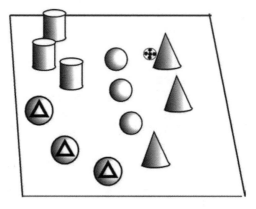

Objective:
Technical: Receiving touch must set up the second touch.
Tactical: Identify passing options when not in possession.

Teaching Points:
1. Push receiving touch to playing space.
2. Keep looking for new passing options.
3. Off-the-ball movement with eyes up to see options.

Set up:
Players: 12 players
Gear: 4 cones, 9 vests (3 colors), 2 goals, balls
Field: 20 yds by 25 yds
Time: 90 minutes

Instructions:
There are four teams of three players each. The game is 9v3 keep away. One of the teams begins as the three defenders. When they win the ball they join the attacking group and the team responsible for losing the ball immediately becomes the defending team. The attacking nine play two touch. Play 20 minutes.

Progression:
The team of three receiving a pass may not pass directly to the team it was received from. The attacking nine play one touch. Play 20 minutes.

Progression:
The touches are now in sequence. The first team receiving a pass plays one touch. The next team must play two touch. The third team must play three touch then repeat sequence. When the defending three wins the ball, the team receiving the next pass begins by playing one touch to another team. Play 20 minutes.

Set up:
> Players: 12 players, 2 goalkeepers
> Gear: 4 cones, 7 vests (2 colors) 2 goals, balls
> Field: 50 yds by 44 yds
> Time: 30 minutes

Progression:
The game is 5v5 plus 2 neutral players to goal. The game is three touch. Both neutral players must get a pass during a team's possession before that team can attack the goal. A goal counts as 1 point. If the scoring team wins the ball back before the opposition makes a pass to a neutral player they may attack goal directly. If they score it counts for 2 points. Play 3 games of 10 minutes each.

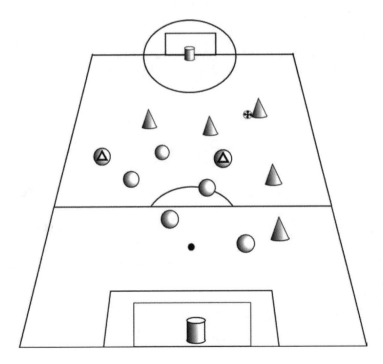

Finishing Via Combination Play

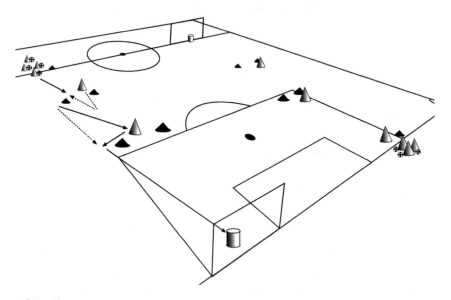

Objective:
> Technical: Shooting first time after a receiving a layoff pass.
> Tactical: Accelerate to the ball then shoot low.

Teaching points:
> 1. Move forward when passing forward.
> 2. Accelerate to the ball after it is laid off.
> 3. Pick target then lock eyes on the ball and shoot.

Set up:
> Players: 12 players, 2 goalkeepers
> Gear: 9 cones, 2 goals, spare balls
> Field: half field
> Time: 90 minutes

Instructions:
The two goals are offset from one another. There are two six foot
wide cone goals 20 and 35 yards in front of each goal. To start, there
is 1 player in each cone goal and 4 players at each starting point. The
starting player takes a dribble then plays a 1-2 with the first layoff
player who has checked back through the cone goal. Another 1-2 is
played with the second checking back layoff player then the shot is

taken to keeper's hands. The shooter then moves to the starting point for the opposite goal. Change the layoff players periodically. Play 10 minutes.

Progression:
The shots are now live. Play 20 minutes.

Progression:
After the starting player plays the first 1-2, the pass is made to the second layoff player who then turns and takes the shot. Each player moves up one position after the shot. Play 20 minutes.

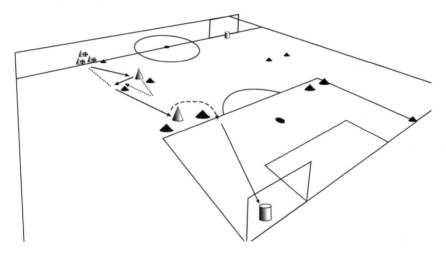

Progression:
The starting player plays the first pass to the second checking back layoff player who passes to the first layoff player. The starting player has continued running and receives the pass into forward space and takes the shot. The players move one position backward after the play and stay on the same goal. Play 20 minutes. (see diagram on following page)

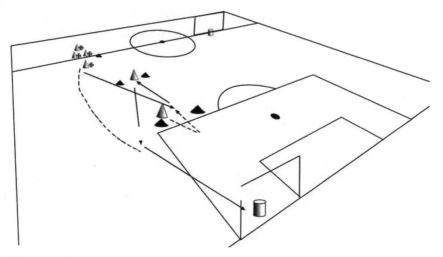

Progression:
Play 6v6 to goal. If a goal results directly from combination play it counts as two points. Play 2 games of 10 minutes each.

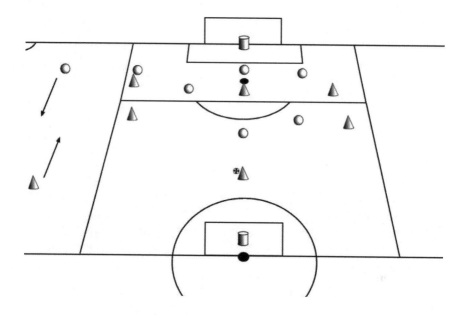

Finishing From Distance

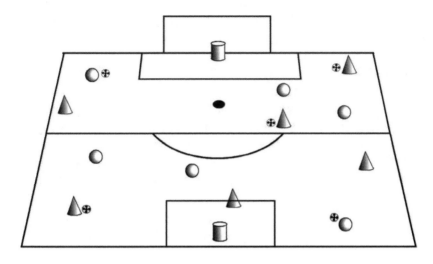

Objectives:
>Technical: Striking a driven ball on target.
>Tactical: Identifying shooting opportunities.

Teaching Points:
>1. Contact the ball on the laces.
>2. Land on the shooting foot
>3. Get in position to shoot from a drop pass.

Set up:
>Players: 12 players, 2 Goalkeepers
>Gear: 6 cones, 6 vests, 5 balls, 2 goals
>Field: 36 yds long by 44 yds wide
>Time: 90 minutes

Instructions:
There are two teams of six players each and a goalkeeper in each goal. The teams combine and pass the five balls to   each other while moving. When a goalkeeper calls a player's name that player strikes the ball firmly to the keeper's hands then follows the shot. The keeper rolls the distribution to another player. Play 10 minutes.

Progression:

After playing to a keeper the player follows the shot to goal. The keeper throws the ball to the player's head and the player attempts to beat the keeper with a head ball. Play 10 minutes.

Progression:

The game is 6v6. Create a 4v2 in each half of the field. The team of four is in their defensive half while their two teammates are in the team's attacking half. Players may not cross over the half line. The two attackers attempt to score against the four defenders. If they elect to make a drop pass to one of their four teammates the player receiving the pass must shoot or pass within two touches. The drop passer and the shooter switch places after a shot. Play 4 games of 5 minutes each.

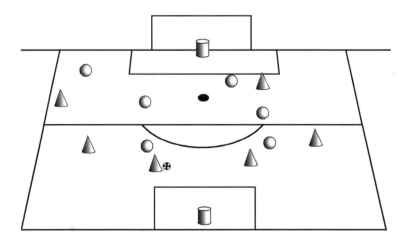

Progression:

The player receiving the drop pass now has the option to dribble the ball over the half line. If the ball is dribbled over the half line, the dribbler must shoot . A teammate of the dribbler transitions to the defensive half. Teams get two points on a goal from the defensive half and one point for a goal from the attacking half. Play 4 games of 5 minutes each.

Progression:
Position the players 3v3 in each half. Defensive players may score by shooting from their own half or dribbling over the half line. Even the numbers back to 3v3 on the fly. The scoring is the same. Play 3 games of 10 minutes each.

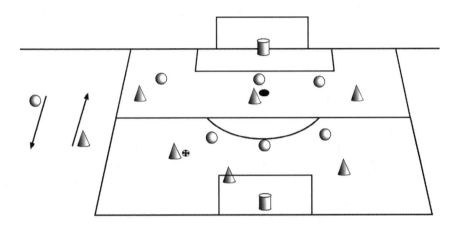

Finishing Off the Turn

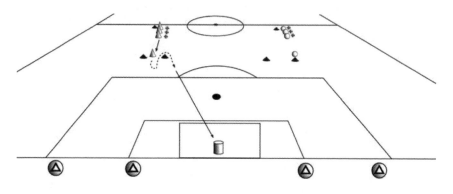

Objective:

Technical: Placement of turning touch to prepare shot.
Tactical: Target the corner the goalkeeper gives the shooter.

Teaching Points:

1. Check back to the ball hard after feint to go forward.
2. The second touch should be a shot.
3. Pick a target corner, shoot and follow.

Set up:

Players: 12 players, 1 goalkeeper
Gear: 6 cones, 8 vests (2 colors), 2 goals, balls
Field: half field
Time: 90 minutes

Instructions:

Two teams of four players work while one team of four retrieves shots that miss the goal and return them to the shooters. A six foot wide cone goal 25 yards from goal is located on each side of the middle of the 18-yard line. To begin, a pass is made from one of the starting players to a player checking back through the cones. That player turns the ball to the inside and play to the goalkeeper's hands. The players move up a position after a shot. Alternate shots and shooters from side to side. Play 3 games of 5 minutes each. Switch the retrieving team each game.

Progression:
The shots after the turn are now live. Play 3 games of 5 minutes each. Keep score.

Progression:
The starting player plays a 1 2-1 with the checking back shooter. The ball must be turned with the outside foot. Play 3 games of 5 minutes each.

Progression:
The shooter is now positioned several feet to the outside of the cone goal. After receiving the ball from the starting player, the shooter plays a pass to himself on the side of the cones further from goal then runs to the ball from goal side of the cones, turns on the ball and shoots. Play 3 games of 5 minutes each.

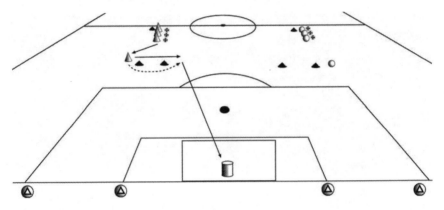

Progression:
Play a game of 5v5 plus 2 neutral players with a second goal which is empty. One team begins with the two neutral players and keeps them until the opposition scores three times in the open goal. The new team of seven now attacks the goal with the goalkeeper. The goals count for two points if scored off a turn. Play 3 games of 10 minutes each.

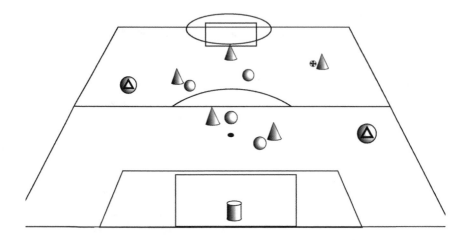

Team Shape in Defense

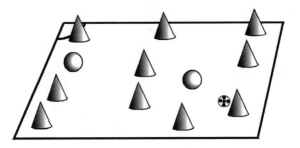

Objectives:

    Technical: Individual defensive posture

    Tactical: Keep the defensive team compact.

Teaching Points:

    1. Proper position to delay a pass played forward.

    2. Move laterally with the ball as it moves.

    3. Prevent passes that split the defenders.

Set up:

    Players: 12 players

    Gear: 4 cones, 2 vests, spare balls

    Field: 18 yds by 15 yds

    Time: 10 minutes

Instructions:

The game is one touch 10v2 keep away. The two defenders hold vests in their hands. When they touch a ball they drop the vest and the last attacker to touch the ball picks up the vest and defends.

Set up:

    Players: 12 players, 2 Goalkeepers

    Gear: 16 cones, 6 vests, 2 goals, balls

    Field: 50 yds by 44 yds. Four vertical channels

    Time: 80 minutes

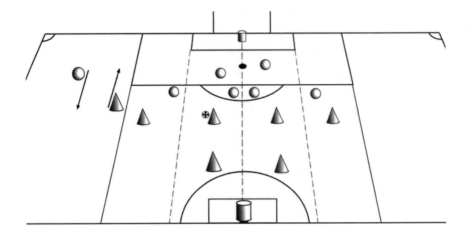

Instructions:
The game is 6v6 to goal. The players are positioned four across the front with two players in the middle channels playing behind them. Players may not leave the channels they are playing in. Play 2 games of 10 minutes each.

Progression:
The two deep players may change zones from side to side when positioned behind their four teammates. If one of them slides over the other must also slide over one zone to follow the first.

When the attacking team has the ball in the widest channel the defender in the opposite wide channel must slide into the next channel and drop in next to a deep player.

Progression:
One team plays under the above movement restrictions while the other may move about the field unrestricted. Play 2 games of 10 minutes each. The teams switch roles for the second game.

Progression:

Both teams move freely within a 2-4 system. Play 2 games of 10 minutes each.

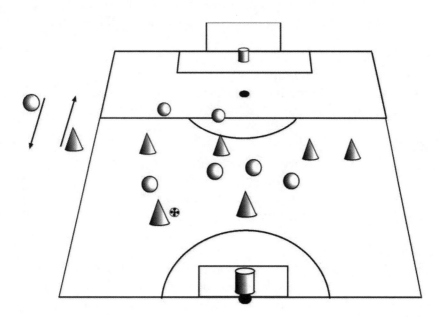

Pressure Defending in Threes

Objective:
> Technical: Moving compactly in a block of three players.
> Tactical: Moving to reduce the opposition's playing area.

Teaching Points:
> 1. First defender quickly pressures the ball.
> 2. Second defender supports first, anticipates pass.
> 3. Third defender plays sweeper behind first two.

Set up:
> Players: 12 players, 1 goalkeeper
> Gear: 6 cones, 6 vests, 2 goals, balls
> Field: 36 yds x 30 yds with halfway line
> Time: 90 minutes

Instructions:
There are two teams of six players each combining together for the warm up. The teams have four balls between them which are passed while moving freely around the field. When the goalkeeper moving freely calls a player's name that player passes to the keeper's feet. The keeper distributes the ball then calls another name. Play 10 minutes.

Progression:
On one half of the field there is a 6v3 with the goalkeeper. The remaining three players are positioned in the opposite half. The team of six begins with the ball and plays two touch keep away. If a player uses an additional touch the pass must go to the goalkeeper's feet. When the team of three wins the ball from the team of six they pass quickly to their teammates in the opposite half. Three players from each team step to the opposite half to create a new 6v3. When the ball is won back the pass back to the original half must go to the keeper's feet. Play 10 games of 2 minutes each. The team possessing the ball at time gets 1 point. (see diagram at top of next page)

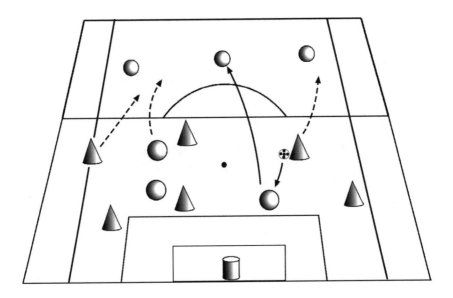

Progression:

The game is now played on the single goal. The game begins 6v3 in the half with the goal. The other three players from the defending team are resting. When the three win the ball they go directly to goal. On a save or dead ball the keeper restarts the game by playing to the team of six. Play each game then have the resting three players join their teammates for a new team of six players. The original team of six has three players rest and three players on the field. Continue to rotate and rest the players while keeping score. Play 2 games of 10 minutes each.

Progression:

If the team of six players completes eight consecutive passes during a possession they may shoot at the goal. If they score it counts for 2 points. Play 2 games of 10 minutes each.

Progression:

The game is now 4v4 with one team resting. The team scoring a goal stays on. The team scored on switches out. On a turnover, the ball winning team must take the ball back behind the half line before attacking goal. The teams must score twice in a row for the point to count. Play 2 games of 10 minutes each.

Pressure Defending

Objective:
Technical: Immediate transition to closing defense.
Tactical: Identify cues to high pressure.

Teaching Points:
1. The nearest player goes immediately to lost ball.
2. Use lines to compress space near the ball.
3. Counter quickly on won ball.

Set up:
Players: 12 players, 2 Goalkeepers
Gear: 6 cones, 6 vests, 2 goals, balls
Field: 50 x 44 yds with a halfway line
Time: 90 minutes

Instructions:
There are two teams of six players each with one ball per team playing on the same half of the field. The teams move around the field playing one touch passes to teammates. Later, change to passing one touch to an opposition player. Play 10 minutes.

Progression:
The game is 6v6 possession. If a team makes five consecutive passes on the same half of the field they score one point then move to the opposite half. One of the passes during the possession must go to the goalkeeper's feet. On a won ball by the defending team they play early to the opposite keeper's feet and all players step to that half and continue the game. Games are to 10 points. Play 20 minutes. (see diagram at top of next page)

Progression:
6v6 to goal. After a team scores a goal they must score again before the opposition does for the point to count. Play 2 games of 10 minutes each.

Progression:
After the first goal has been scored, the next team to score gets the point. Play 2 games of 10 minutes each.

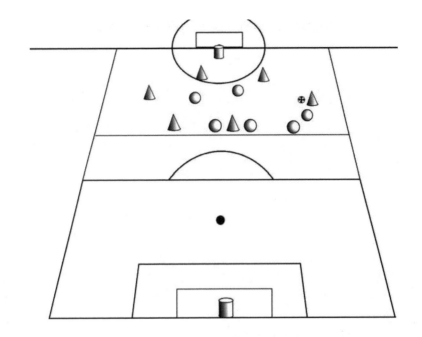

Progression:
After a goal is scored, if the scoring team doesn't get the ball back from the opposition within five passes the goal does not count. Play 4 games of 5 minutes each.

Defending Near the Opponent's Goal

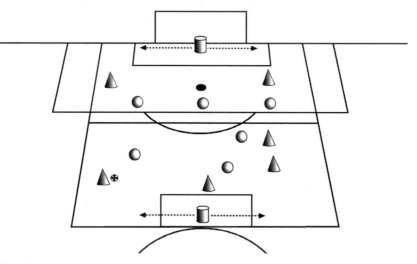

Objectives:

    Technical: Shooting early on a won ball near goal.

    Tactical: Close tightly as a unit toward the ball at speed.

Teaching Points:

    1. Nearest player to the ball stops forward pass.

    2. Move quickly to mark players/space near ball.

    3. Keep depth to win weak panic clears.

Set up:

    Players:12 players, 2 goalkeepers

    Gear: 14 cones, 6 vests, spare balls

    Field: 40 yds by 30 yds with halfway line

    Time: 90 minutes

Instructions:

The game is 6v6 possession. The defending team is allowed to play with their hands to win balls. After catching a ball the player must throw a pass that changes the point of attack. The team that lost the ball may now use their hands. A point is scored after a successful combination play with both goalkeepers during the same possession. Play 4 games of 5 minutes each.

Progression:
The game is now to goal. When the defending team wins the ball in their own half they must pass to their own goalkeeper before attacking goal. The goalkeeper must abide by match rules. Play 2 games of 10 minutes each.

Progression:
There are now two five yard cone goals on each side of the big goals in each half. If on a won ball the defending team is able to dribble or pass forward through a cone goal in their own half they get one point. A ball scored in a big goal is worth two points. A ball scored in the big goal directly after scoring on a cone goal is worth three points. Play 3 games of 10 minutes each.

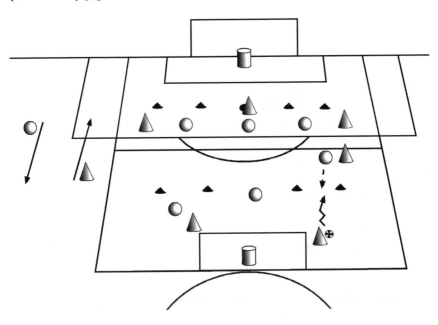

Progression:
Play to the two big goals. A goal is one point. A goal on a ball won in the opponent's half is worth two points. Play 2 games of 10 minutes each.

Man to Man Defending

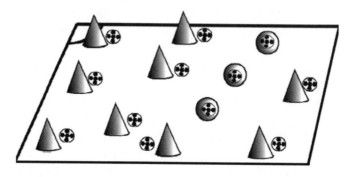

Objectives:
> Technical: Quick footwork to mark an attacker.
> Tactical: Denying passing angles to attackers.

Teaching points:
> 1. Stay in touching distance of an attacker.
> 2. See the ball and the attacker.
> 3. Play away from pressure on a won ball.

Set up:
> Players: 12 players
> Gear: 4 cones, 12 balls
> Field: 18 yds by 15 yds
> Time: 20 minutes

Instructions:
The game is tag. Three of the twelve players are "it". They carry their balls in their hands while the other nine players have balls at their feet. When an "it" player tags one of the nine players the tagged player picks their ball and becomes an "it" player while the former "it" player drops the ball and becomes a dribbler. Play 10 games of 1 minute each. The three "it" players at time must do three forward rolls each to signal the start of the next game.

Progression:

If two players make physical contact with each other they are safe from being tagged. The "it" player must move to someone else and the two players release each other and continue moving. Play 10 games of 1 minute each. The three "it" players at the time must run five tight circles around their ball to signal the start of the next game.

Set up:

Players: 12 players
Gear: 4 cones, 6 vests, spare balls
Field: 40 yds by 30 yds
Time: 40 minutes

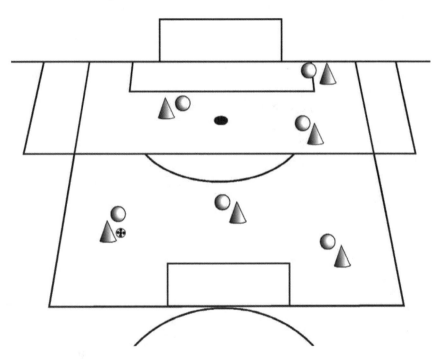

Instructions:

The game is 6v6 possession. There are six pairs of assigned lvl's. Each pair must defend each other only. There is no leaving your man to double team the ball. Play a four or five touch maximum per player. Play 10 games of 2 minutes each. The team with the ball at time get one point. Switch the match ups each game.

Progression:
In the lvl assignments the players will not be marking the same player marking them. On a turnover the losing team will immediately
move to mark their assigned players. Play 10 games of 2 minutes
each. The team with the ball at time get one point.

Progression:
The game is 6v6 to goal. The defending team must win the ball five
times before they become attackers and can go to goal. On a won
ball by the defense the game restarts with throw from the attacking
team's goalkeeper. Play 6 games of 5 minutes each.